MATHEMATICS IN THE PRIMARY SCHOOL

RICHARD R. SKEMP

The Author

Richard R. Skemp is internationally recognized as a leading authority in mathematical education, and has lectured on this subject at 45 universities in seventeen countries, and at many conferences and in-service courses for teachers. Himself a former teacher, he has worked closely with both primary and secondary teachers while developing a theory of intelligent learning which relates closely to classroom needs. His previous books in this field include *The Psychology of Learning Mathematics* (1971), *Intelligence, Learning, and Action* (1979), and *Structured Activities for Primary Mathematics* (1989).

Subjects in the Primary School
Series editor: Professor John Eggleston

MATHEMATICS IN THE PRIMARY SCHOOL

RICHARD R. SKEMP
Emeritus Professor
University of Warwick

London

First published in 1989
by Routledge
11 New Fetter Lane, London EC4P 4EE

Reprinted 2002 by RoutledgeFalmer

RoutledgeFalmer is an imprint of the Taylor & Francis Group

Transferred to Digital Printing 2003

Filmset by Mayhew Typesetting, Bristol

British Library Cataloguing in Publication Data

Skemp, Richard R. (Richard Rowland), 1919–
   Mathematics in the primary school. —
   (Subjects in the primary school).
   1. Primary schools. Curriculum subjects :
   Mathematics. Teaching
   I. Title   II. Series
   372.7' 3044

ISBN 0-415-02519-2

Contents

Acknowledgements

Most of the contents of this book has been presented orally over a number of years at in-service courses and conferences for teachers in England and Wales, Germany, Canada, and the United States. The discussions which took place on these occasions have been of great value to me in developing the relations between theory and classroom practice, and I am most grateful to all the teachers, advisers, and lecturers who took part in these; and also to those who initiated, planned, and organised the arrangements which brought us together and helped our work go smoothly.

The classroom activities in Chapters 6 and 7 are taken from a much larger collection developed in the Primary Mathematics Project. This was funded jointly over a period of seven years by the Nuffield Foundation and the Leverhulme Trust, and I am most grateful for their support.

The prologue 'Relational understanding and instrumental understanding' first appeared as an article in the journal *Mathematics Teaching*. Much of Chapter 9, as well as a smaller amount elsewhere in the present book, first appeared in *The Psychology of Learning Mathematics, Expanded American Edition*, published by Lawrence Erlbaum Associates, New Jersey. My cordial thanks to the editors concerned for agreeing to the inclusion of this material.

Prologue: Relational understanding and instrumental understanding

This prologue first appeared in 1976, as an article in the journal Mathematics Teaching.[1] *It has since been reproduced three times, and read and discussed in three continents. During this time the terms 'relational understanding' and 'instrumental understanding' have become part of the language of mathematics education. It is hoped that present readers too will find these ideas a helpful starting point for their own thinking.*

Throughout the rest of the book, 'understanding' by itself means relational understanding. It will be seen that relational understanding corresponds to intelligent learning, and instrumental understanding to habit learning.

Faux amis

Faux amis is a term used by the French to describe words which are the same, or very alike, in two languages, but whose meanings are different. For example:

French word	Meaning in English
histoire	story, not history
librairie	bookshop, not library
chef	head of an organization, not only chief cook
agrément	pleasure or amusement, not agreement
docteur	doctor (higher degree), not medical practitioner
médecin	medical practitioner, not medicine
parent	relations in general, including parents

One gets *faux amis* between English as spoken in different parts of the world. An Englishman asking in America for a biscuit would be given what we call a scone. To get what we call a biscuit, he would have to ask for a cookie. And between English as used in mathematics and in everyday life there are such *faux amis* as field, group, ring, ideal.

A person who is unaware that the word he is using is a *faux ami* can make inconvenient mistakes. We expect history to be true, but not a story. We take books without paying from a library, but not from a bookshop; and so on. But in the foregoing examples there are cues which might put one on guard: difference of language, or of country or of context.

If, however, the word is used in the same language, country and context, with two meanings whose difference is as basic as the difference between (say) the meanings of 'history' and 'histoire' (which is a difference between fact and fiction) one may expect serious confusion.

Two such words can be identified in the context of mathematics; and it is the alternative meaning attached to each of these words, by a large following, which in my belief is at the root of many of the difficulties in mathematics education today.

One of the words is 'understanding'. It was brought to my attention some years ago by Stieg Mellin-Olsen, of Bergen University, that there are in current use two meanings of this word. These he distinguishes by calling them 'relational understanding' and 'instrumental understanding'. By the former is meant what I, and probably most readers of this article, have always meant by understanding: knowing both what to do and why. Instrumental understanding I would until recently not have regarded as understanding at all. It is what I have in the past described as 'rules without reasons', without realizing that for many pupils and their teachers the possession of such a rule, and ability to use it, is what they mean by 'understanding'.

Suppose that a teacher reminds a class that the area of a rectangle is given by $A = L \times B$. A pupil who has been away says he does not understand, so the teacher gives him an explanation along these lines: 'The formula tells you that to get the area of a rectangle, you multiply the length by the breadth.' 'Oh, I see,' says the child, and gets on with the exercise. If we were now to say to him (in effect), 'You may think you understand, but you don't really,' he would not agree. 'Of course I do. Look, I've got all these answers right.' Nor would he be pleased at our devaluing of his achievement. And within his meaning of the word, he does understand.

We can all think of examples of this kind: 'borrowing' in subtraction, 'turn it upside down and multiply' for division by a fraction, 'take it over to the other side and change the sign' are obvious ones; but once the concept has been formed, other examples of instrumental explanations can be identified in abundance in many widely used texts. Here are two from a text used by a former direct-grant grammar school, now independent, with a high academic standard.

Multiplication of fractions. To multiply a fraction by a fraction, multiply the two numerators together to make the numerator of the product, and the two denominators to make its denominator.

e.g. $\dfrac{2}{3}$ of $\dfrac{4}{5} = \dfrac{2 \times 4}{3 \times 5} = \dfrac{8}{15}$

$\dfrac{3}{5} \times \dfrac{10}{13} = \dfrac{30}{65} = \dfrac{6}{13}$

The multiplication sign $\times$ is generally used instead of the word 'of'.

Circles. The circumference of a circle (that is its perimeter, or the length of its boundary) is found by measurement to be a little more than three times the length of its diameter. In any circle the circumference is approximately 3.1416 times the diameter, which is roughly $3\frac{1}{7}$ times the diameter. Neither of these figures is exact as the exact number cannot be expressed either as a fraction or a decimal. The number is represented by the Greek letter π (pi).

Circumference $= \pi d$ or $2\pi r$
Area $= \pi r^2$

The reader is urged to try for himself this exercise of looking for and identifying examples of instrumental explanations, both in texts and in the classroom. This will have three benefits. (i) For persons like the writer, and most readers of this article, it may provide evidence of what otherwise they would not realize: how widespread is the instrumental approach. (ii) It will help, by repeated examples, to consolidate the two contrasting concepts. (iii) It is a good preparation for trying to formulate the difference in general terms.

If it is accepted that these two categories are both well-filled, by those pupils and teachers whose goals are respectively relational and instrumental understanding (by the pupil), two questions arise. First, does this matter? And second, is one kind of understanding better than the other? For years I have taken for granted the answers to both these questions: briefly, 'Yes; relational.' But the existence of a large body of experienced teachers and of a large number of texts belonging to the opposite camp has forced me to think more about why I hold this view. In the process of changing the judgement from an intuitive to a reflective one, I think I have learnt something useful. The two questions are not entirely separate, but in the present section I shall concentrate as far as possible on the first: does it matter?

The problem here is that of a mis-match, which arises automatically in any *faux amis* situation, and does not depend on whether A's or B's meaning 'is the right one'. Let us imagine, if we can, that school A send a team to play school B at a game called 'football', but that neither team knows that there are two kinds (called 'association' and 'rugby'). School A plays soccer and has never heard of rugger, and vice versa for B. Each team will rapidly decide that the others are crazy, or a lot of foul players. Team A in particular will think that team B players use a mis-shapen ball, and commit one foul after another. Unless the two sides stop and talk about what game they think they are playing at, the game will break up in disorder and the two teams will never want to meet again.

Though it may be hard to imagine such a situation arising on the football field, this is not a far-fetched analogy for what goes on in many mathematics lessons, even now. There is this important difference, that one side at least cannot refuse to play. The encounter is compulsory, on five days a week, for about thirty-six weeks a year, over ten years or more of a child's life.

Leaving aside for the moment whether one kind of understanding is better than the other, there are two kinds of mathematical mis-match which can occur.

1 Pupils whose goal is to understand instrumentally, taught by a teacher who wants them to understand relationally.
2 The other way about.

The first of these will cause fewer problems *short-term* to the pupils, though it will be frustrating for the teacher. The pupils just 'won't want to know' all the careful groundwork he gives in preparation for whatever is to be learnt next, nor his careful explanations. All they want is some kind of rule for getting the answer. As soon as this is reached, they latch on to it and ignore the rest.

If the teacher asks a question that does not quite fit the rule, of course they will get it wrong. For the following example I have to thank Mr Peter Burney, at that time a student at Coventry College of Education on teaching practice. While teaching area he became suspicious that the children did not really understand what they were doing. So he asked them: 'What is the area of a field 20 cms by 15 yards?' The reply was: '300 square centimetres.' He asked: 'Why not 300 square yards?' Answer: 'Because area is always in square centimetres.'

To prevent errors like the above the pupils need another rule (or, of course, relational understanding), that both dimensions must be in the same unit. This anticipates one of the arguments which I shall use against instrumental understanding, that it usually involves a multiplicity of rules rather than fewer principles of more general application.

There is of course always the chance that a few of the pupils will catch on to what the teacher is trying to do. If only for the sake of these, the effort should be maintained. But by many, probably a majority, attempts to convince them that being able to use the rule is not enough will not be well received. 'Well is the enemy of better', and if pupils can get the right answer by the kind of thinking they are used to, they will not take kindly to suggestions that they should try for something beyond this.

The other mis-match, in which pupils are trying to understand relationally but the teaching makes this impossible, can be a more damaging one. An instance which stays in my memory is that of a neighbour's child, then seven years old. He was a very bright little boy, with an I.Q. of 140. At the age of five he could read *The Times*, but at seven he regularly cried over his mathematics homework. His misfortune was that he was trying to understand relationally teaching which could not be understood in this way. My evidence for this belief is that when I taught him relationally myself, with the help of Unifix, he caught on quickly and with real pleasure.

A less obvious mis-match is that which may occur between teacher and text. Suppose that we have a teacher whose conception of understanding is instrumental, who for one reason or other is using a text which aims for relational understanding by the pupil. It will take more than this to change his teaching style. I was in a school which was using my own text,[2] and noticed (they were at Chapter 1 of Book 1) that some of the pupils were writing answers like:

'the set of {flowers}'

When I mentioned this to the teacher (he was head of mathematics) he asked the class to pay attention to him and said: 'Some of you are not writing your answers properly. Look at the example in the book, at the beginning of the exercise, and be sure you write your answers like that.'

Much of what is being taught under the description of 'modern mathematics' is being taught and learnt just as instrumentally as were the syllabi which have been replaced. This is predictable from the difficulty we normally experience in accommodating (restructuring) our existing schemas.[3] To the extent that this is so, the innovations have probably done more harm than good, by introducing a mis-match between the teacher and the aims implicit in the new content. For the purpose of introducing ideas such as sets, mappings and variables is the help which, rightly used, they can give to relational understanding. If pupils are still being taught instrumentally, then a 'traditional' syllabus will probably benefit them more. They will at least acquire proficiency in a number of mathematical techniques which will be of use to them in other subjects, and the lack of which has recently been the subject of complaints by teachers of science, employers and others.

Near the beginning of this chapter I said that two major *faux amis* could be identified in the context of mathematics. The second one is even more troublesome; it is the word 'mathematics' itself. For we are not talking about better and worse teaching of the same kind of mathematics. It is easy to think this, just as our imaginary soccer players who do not know that their opponents are playing a different game might think that the other side pick up the ball and run with it because they cannot kick properly, especially with such a mis-shapen ball – in which case they might kindly offer them a better ball and some lessons in dribbling. It has taken me some time to realize that this is not the case.

I used to think that maths teachers were all teaching the same subject, some doing it better than others. I now believe that *there are two effectively different subjects being taught under the same name, 'mathematics'*. If this is true, then this difference matters beyond any of the differences in syllabi which are so widely debated. So I would like to try to emphasize the point with the help of another analogy.

Imagine that two groups of children are taught music as a pencil-and-paper subject. They are all shown the five-line stave, with the curly 'treble' sign at the beginning; and taught that marks on the lines are called E, G, B, D, F. Marks between the lines are called F, A, C, E. They learn that a mark with an open oval is called a minim, and is worth two marks with blacked-in ovals which are called crotchets, or four with blacked-in ovals and a tail which are called quavers, and so on – musical multiplication tables if you like. For one group of children, all their learning is of this kind and nothing beyond. If they have a music lesson a day, five days a week in school terms, and are told that it is important, these children could in time probably learn to write out the marks for simple melodies such as those for 'God Save the Queen', and 'Auld Lang Syne', and to solve simple problems such as 'What time is this in?' and 'What key?', and even 'Transpose this melody from C major to G major.' They would find it boring, and the rules to be memorized would be so numerous that problems like 'Write a simple accompaniment for this melody' would be too difficult for most. They would give up the subject as soon as possible, and remember it with dislike.

The other group is taught to associate certain sounds with the marks on paper. For the first few years these are audible sounds, which they make themselves on simple instruments. After a time they can still imagine the sounds whenever they see or write the marks on paper. Associated with every linear sequence of marks is a melody, and with every vertical set a harmony. The keys C major and G major have an audible relationship, and a similar relationship can be found between certain other pairs of keys. And so on. Much less memory work is involved, and what has to be remembered is largely in the form of related wholes (such as melodies) which their minds easily retain. Exercises such as were mentioned earlier ('Write a simple accompaniment') would be within the ability of most. These children would also find their learning intrinsically pleasurable, and many would continue it voluntarily, even after O-level or C.S.E.

For the present purpose I have invented two non-existent kinds of 'music lesson', both pencil-and-paper exercises (in the second case, after the first year or two). But the difference between these imaginary activities is no greater than that between two activities which actually go under the name of mathematics. (We can make the analogy closer, if we imagine that the first group of children were initially taught sounds for the notes in a rather half-hearted way, but that the associations were too ill-formed and unorganized to last.)

The above analogy is, clearly, heavily biased in favour of relational mathematics. This reflects my own viewpoint. To call it a viewpoint, however, implies that I no longer regard it as a self-evident truth which requires no justification: which it can hardly be if many experienced teachers continue to teach instrumental mathematics. The next step is to try to argue the merits of both points of view as clearly and fairly as possible; and especially of the point of view opposite to one's own. This is why the next section is called 'Devil's advocate'.

Devil's advocate

Given that so many teachers teach instrumental mathematics, might this be because it does have certain advantages? I have been able to think of three advantages (as distinct from situational reasons for teaching this way, which will be discussed later).

1 Within its own context, *instrumental mathematics is usually easier to understand*; sometimes much easier. Some topics, such as multiplying two negative numbers together, or dividing by a fractional number, are difficult to understand relationally. 'Minus times minus equals plus', and 'To divide by a fraction you turn it upside down and multiply' are easily remembered rules. If what is wanted is a page of right answers, instrumental mathematics can provide this more quickly and easily.

2 *So the rewards are more immediate, and more apparent.* It is nice to get a page of right answers, and we must not under-rate the importance of the feeling of success which pupils get from this.[4] Recently I visited a school where some of the children described themselves as 'thickos'. Their teachers used the term too. These children need success to restore their self-confidence, and it can be argued that they can achieve this more quickly and easily in instrumental mathematics than in relational.

3 Just because less knowledge is involved, *one can often get the right answer more quickly and reliably* by instrumental thinking than relational. This difference is so marked that even relational mathematicians often use instrumental thinking.[5] This is a point of much theoretical interest, which I hope to discuss more fully on a future occasion.

The above may well not do full justice to instrumental mathematics. I shall be glad to know of any further advantages which it may have.

The case for relational mathematics

There are four advantages (at least) in relational mathematics.

1 *It is more adaptable to new tasks.* Recently I was trying

to help a boy who had learnt to multiply two decimal fractions together by dropping the decimal point, multiplying as for whole numbers, and re-inserting the decimal point to give the same total number of digits after the decimal point as there were before. This is a handy method if you know why it works. Through no fault of his own, this child did not; and not unreasonably, applied it also to division of decimals. By this method 4.8 ÷ 0.6 came to 0.08. The same pupil had also learnt that if you know two angles of a triangle, you can find the third by adding the two given angles together and subtracting from 180°. He got ten questions right this way (his teacher believed in plenty of practice), and went on to use the same method for finding the exterior angles. So he got the next five answers wrong.

I do not think he was being stupid in either of these cases. He was simply extrapolating from what he already knew. But relational understanding, by knowing not only what method worked but why, would have enabled him to relate the method to new problems. Instrumental mathematics necessitates memorizing which problems a method works for and which not, and also learning a different method for each new class of problems. So the first advantage of relational mathematics leads to:

2 *It is easier to remember.* There is a seeming paradox here, in that it is certainly harder to learn. It is certainly easier for pupils to learn that 'area of a triangle $= \frac{1}{2}$ base $\times$ height' than to learn why this is so. But they then have to learn separate rules for triangles, rectangles, parallelograms, trapeziums; whereas relational understanding consists partly in seeing all of these in relation to the area of a rectangle. It is still desirable to know the separate rules; one does not want to have to derive them afresh every time.[6] But knowing also how they are inter-related enables one to remember them as parts of a connected whole, which is easier. There is more to learn – the connections as well as the separate rules – but the result, once learnt, is more lasting. So there is less re-learning to do, and long-term the time taken may well be less altogether.

Teaching for relational understanding may also involve more actual content. Earlier, an instrumental explanation was quoted leading to the statement 'Circumference = πd'. For relational understanding of this, the idea of a proportion would have to be taught first (among others), and this would make it a much longer job than simply teaching the rules as given. But proportionality has such a wide range of other applications that it is worth teaching on these grounds also. In relational mathematics this happens rather often. Ideas required for understanding a particular topic turn out to be basic for understanding many other topics too. Sets, mappings and equivalence are such ideas. Unfortunately their potential benefits are often lost by teaching them as separate topics, rather than as fundamental concepts by which whole areas of mathematics can be inter-related.

3 *Relational knowledge can be effective as a goal in itself.* This is an empiric fact, based on evidence from controlled experiments using non-mathematical material. The need for external rewards and punishments is greatly reduced, making what is often called the 'motivational' side of a teacher's job much easier. This is related to:

4 *Relational schemas are organic in quality.* This is the best way I have been able to formulate a quality by which they seem to act as agents of their own growth. The connection with 3 is that if people get satisfaction from relational understanding, they may not only try to understand relationally new material which is put before them, but also actively seek out new material and explore new areas, very much like a tree extending its roots or an animal exploring new territory in search of nourishment. To develop this idea beyond the level of an analogy is beyond the scope of the present paper, but it is too important to leave out.

If the above is anything like a fair presentation of the arguments for each side, it would appear that while a case might exist for instrumental mathematics short-term and with a limited context, long-term and in the context of a child's

11

whole education it does not. So why are so many children taught only instrumental mathematics throughout their school careers? Unless we can answer this, there is little hope of improving the situation.

An individual teacher might make a reasoned choice to teach for instrumental understanding on one or more of the following grounds.

1 That relational understanding would take too long to achieve, and to be able to use a particular technique is all that these pupils are likely to need.
2 That relational understanding of a particular topic is too difficult, but the pupils still need to learn the topic for examination reasons.
3 That a skill is needed for use in another subject (e.g. science) before it can be understood relationally with schemas currently available to the pupils.
4 That he is a junior teacher in a school where all the other mathematics teaching is instrumental.

All of these imply, as does the phrase 'make a reasoned choice', that he is able to consider the alternative goals of instrumental and relational understanding on their merits and in relation to a particular situation. To make an informed choice of this kind implies awareness of the distinction, and relational understanding of the mathematics itself. So nothing else but relational understanding can be adequate for a teacher. One has to face the fact that this is absent in many who teach mathematics; perhaps even a majority.

Situational factors which contribute to the difficulty include:

1 *The backwash effect of examinations.* In view of the importance of examinations for future employment, one can hardly blame pupils if success in these is one of their major aims. The way pupils work cannot but be influenced by the goal for which they are working, which is to answer correctly a sufficient number of questions.[7]
2 *Over-burdened syllabi.* Part of the trouble here is the high concentration of the information content of mathematics. A mathematical statement may condense

into a single line as much as in another subject might take over one or two paragraphs. By mathematicians accustomed to handling such concentrated ideas, this is often overlooked (which may be why most mathematics lecturers go too fast). Non-mathematicians do not realize it at all. Whatever the reason, almost all syllabi would be much better if much reduced in amount so that there would be time to teach them better.

3 *Difficulty of assessment of whether a person understands relationally or instrumentally.* From the marks he makes on paper, it is very hard to make valid inference about the mental processes by which a pupil has been led to make them; hence the difficulty of sound examining in mathematics. In a teaching situation, talking with the pupil is almost certainly the best way to find out; but in a class of over thirty, it may be difficult to find the time.

4 *The great psychological difficulty for teachers of accommodating (re-structuring) their existing and long-standing schemas,* even for the minority who know the need to, want to do so, and have time for study.

From a recent article discussing the practical, intellectual and cultural value of mathematics education (and I have no doubt that he means relational mathematics!) by Sir Hermann Bondi, I take these three paragraphs. (In the original, they are not consecutive.)

So far my glowing tribute to mathematics has left out a vital point: the rejection of mathematics by so many, a rejection that in not a few cases turns to abject fright.

The negative attitude to mathematics, unhappily so common, even among otherwise highly-educated people is surely the greatest measure of our failure and a real danger to our society.

This is perhaps the clearest indication that something is wrong, and indeed very wrong, with the situation. It is not hard to blame education for at least a share of the responsibility; it is harder to pinpoint the blame, and even more difficult to suggest new remedies.[8]

If for 'blame' we may substitute 'cause', there can be small doubt that the widespread failure to teach relational mathematics – a failure to be found in primary, secondary and further education, and in 'modern' as well as 'traditional' courses – can be identified as a major cause. To suggest new remedies is indeed difficult, but it may be hoped that diagnosis is one good step towards a cure. Another step will be offered in the next section.

A theoretical formulation

There is nothing so powerful for directing one's actions in a complex situation, and for co-ordinating one's own efforts with those of others, as a good theory. All good teachers build up their own stores of empirical knowledge, and have abstracted from these some general principles on which they rely for guidance. But while their knowledge remains in this form it is largely still at the intuitive level within individuals, and cannot be communicated, both for this reason and because there is no shared conceptual structure (schema) in terms of which it can be formulated. Were this possible, individual efforts could be integrated into a unified body of knowledge which would be available for use by newcomers to the profession. At present most teachers have to learn from their own mistakes.

For some time my own comprehension of the difference between the two kinds of learning which lead respectively to relational and instrumental mathematics remained at the intuitive level, though I was personally convinced that the difference was one of great importance, and this view was shared by most of those with whom I discussed it. Awareness of the need for an explicit formulation was forced on me in the course of two parallel research projects; and insight came, quite suddenly, during a recent conference. Once seen it appears quite simple, and one wonders why I did not think of it before. But there are two kinds of simplicity: that of naïvety; and that which, by penetrating beyond superficial differences, brings simplicity by unifying. It is the second kind which a good theory has to offer, and this is harder to achieve.

A concrete example is necessary to begin with. When I went

to stay in a certain town for the first time, I quickly learnt several particular routes. I learnt to get between where I was staying and the office of the colleague with whom I was working; between where I was staying and the university refectory where I ate; between my friend's office and the refectory; and two or three others. In brief, I learnt a limited number of fixed plans by which I could get from particular starting locations to particular goal locations.

As soon as I had some free time I began to explore the town. Now I was not wanting to get anywhere specific, but to learn my way around, and in the process to see what I might come upon that was of interest. At this stage my goal was a different one: to construct in my mind a cognitive map of the town.

These two activities are quite different. Nevertheless they are, to an outside observer, difficult to distinguish. Anyone seeing me walk from A to B would have great difficulty in knowing (without asking me) which of the two I was engaged in. But the most important thing about an activity is its goal. In one case my goal was to get to B, which is a physical location. In the other it was to enlarge or consolidate my mental map of the town, which is a state of knowledge.

A person with a set of fixed plans can find his way from a certain set of starting points to a certain set of goals. The characteristic of a plan is that it tells him what to do at each choice point: turn right out of the door, go straight on past the church, and so on. But if at any stage he makes a mistake, he will be lost; and he will stay lost if he is not able to retrace his steps and get back on the right path.

In contrast, a person with a mental map of the town has something from which he can produce, when needed, an almost infinite number of plans by which he can guide his steps from any starting point to any finishing point, provided only that both can be imagined on his mental map. And if he does take a wrong turn, he will still know where he is, and thereby be able to correct his mistake without getting lost; even perhaps to learn from it.

The analogy between the foregoing and the learning of mathematics is close. The kind of learning which leads to instrumental mathematics consists of the learning of an increasing number of fixed plans, by which pupils can find their way from particular starting points (the data) to required finishing points (the answers to the questions). The plan tells them what to do at each choice point, as in the concrete example. And as in the concrete example, *what has to be done next is determined purely by the local situation.* ('When you see the post office, turn left.' 'When you have cleared brackets, collect like terms.') There is no awareness of the overall relationship between successive stages, and the final goal. And in both cases, the learner is dependent on outside guidance for learning each new 'way to get there'.

In contrast, learning relational mathematics consists of building up a conceptual structure (schema) from which its possessor can (in principle) produce an unlimited number of plans for getting from any starting point within his schema to any finishing point. (I say 'in principle' because of course some of these paths will be much harder to construct than others.)

This kind of learning is different in several ways from instrumental learning.

1 The means become independent of particular ends to be reached thereby.
2 Building up a schema within a given area of knowledge becomes an intrinsically satisfying goal in itself.
3 The more complete a pupil's schema, the greater his feeling of confidence in his own ability to find new ways of 'getting there' without outside help.
4 But a schema is never complete. As our schemas enlarge, so our awareness of possibilities is thereby enlarged.
  Thus the process often becomes self-continuing, and (by virtue of 3) self-rewarding.

Taking again for a moment the role of devil's advocate, it is fair to ask whether we are indeed talking about two subjects, relational mathematics and instrumental mathematics, or just two ways of thinking about the same subject matter. Using my earlier analogy, the two processes described might be regarded as two different ways of knowing about the same town; in which case the distinction made between relational and instrumental understanding would be valid, but not that between instrumental and relational mathematics.

But what constitutes mathematics is not the subject matter, but a particular kind of knowledge about it. The subject matter of relational and instrumental mathematics may be the same: cars travelling at uniform speeds between two towns, towers whose heights are to be found, bodies falling freely under gravity, etc. etc. But the two kinds of knowledge are so different that I think that there is a strong case for regarding them as different kinds of mathematics. If this distinction is accepted, then the word 'mathematics' is for many children indeed a false friend, as they find to their cost.

Part A

1

Why is mathematics still a problem subject for so many?

Evidence from surveys: a vote of no confidence

In the United Kingdom, ever since the early 1960s, there have been intensive efforts to improve mathematical education in our schools, by many intelligent, hard-working, and well-funded persons. Nevertheless, in the late 1970s, the state of mathematical education in our schools was still such as to give cause for concern at governmental level. This led to the setting up of a governmental Committee of Enquiry, whose meetings continued over a period of three years. The first stage of this inquiry consisted of interviews with people chosen to represent a stratified sample of the population. One of the most striking things about these interviews is those which did not take place.

> Both direct and indirect approaches were tried, the word 'mathematics' was replaced by 'arithmetic' or 'everyday use of numbers' but it was clear that the reason for people's refusal to be interviewed was simply that the subject was mathematics . . . This apparently widespread perception amongst adults of mathematics as a daunting subject pervaded a great deal of the sample selection; half of the people approached as being appropriate for inclusion in the sample refused to take part.[1]

Such had been the result, for them, of ten years of so-called mathematical education while at school. As the same report rightly observes:

> Most important of all is the need to have sufficient
> confidence to make effective use of whatever skill and
> understanding is possessed whether this be little or much.[2]

Professor John Eggleston has commented,

> Yet aspiration of this kind is not new . . . a major task is
> to break the patterns of error by both pupils and teachers
> that characterize much of the work in the 'new' as well as
> in 'traditional' mathematics, and which are so destructive of
> confidence in both teachers and taught.[3]

Many of the mathematical errors have been described in
great detail in a report of more than 900 pages from the
Assessment of Performance Unit of the Department of Education and Science.[4] This report makes interesting, though not
encouraging, reading. For example, 31 per cent – almost one
third – of eleven-year-olds tested did not know in which of the
following numbers the 7 stands for 7 tens: 107, 71, 7, 710.
This and other factual surveys (e.g. that of the CSMS group at
Chelsea College, University of London)[5] are valuable in bringing the problem to our attention forcibly and in detail. But
what they do not tell us is why so many children still make
mistakes of this kind after five years of schooling.

Readers in other countries must decide for themselves to
what extent a similar situation exists there. Such information
as I have suggests that the problem is not confined to the
United Kingdom. A distinguished American professor of
mathematics, Dr Hassler Whitney, who is Past President of the
International Commission on Mathematical Instruction and
who has written and spoken extensively in recent years on the
teaching of mathematics to young children, has written:

> For several decades we have been seeing increasing failure
> in school mathematics education, in spite of intensive
> efforts in many directions to improve matters. It should be
> very clear that we are missing something fundamental
> about the schooling process. But we do not even seem to
> be sincerely interested in this; we push for 'excellence'
> without regard for causes of failure or side effects of
> interventions; we try to cure symptoms in place of finding

the underlying disease, and we focus on the passing of tests instead of meaningful goals.[6]

So where, after more than twenty years of attempted reforms, are we still going wrong? If we cannot find at least a partial answer to this question, there is no reason to expect that future efforts will be any more successful than past. One thing must by now be clear, that changes in syllabus are not in themselves sufficient. It would be reasonable also to suspect that the causes are fundamental in the ways children learn mathematics, and therefore in whatever are the factors which affect this, including (but not only) the ways in which they are taught.

I don't think that there is a single answer to the problem, nor that any one person knows all the answers. As my own contribution to progress, I have three answers to offer. The present book centres on two of these: how children learn, and the teaching situation. These are the most fundamental, and are moreover the aspects which teachers are likely to be in a position to remedy, individually and collectively. They also offer a starting point from which we may hope to find some of the other answers.

The need for a new perspective

It seems clear that the problems of mathematical education cannot be solved from within mathematics itself. A wider perspective is needed, which I myself reached only by a long and roundabout path. I hope that this book will help readers to get there more quickly and directly; and although 'there is no royal road',[7] those who make the journey will find it an interesting and rewarding one, quite apart from the professional importance of the goal. As a preliminary, a few lines about my own journey are necessary.

The English poet John Betjeman once said that the best way to appreciate London is to take a journey round the world, starting in London and finishing in London. My own journey has been a mental journey, taking more than thirty years. It began in, and has returned to, the mathematics classroom. But on the way it led through the areas of developmental

23

psychology, motivation, human emotions, cybernetics, evolution, and human intelligence. Eventually it led me to reformulate my own conception of human intelligence, at which point I found myself, unexpectedly, back at mathematics again.

This journey was largely a quest for solutions of two problems, one professional and one theoretical. The professional problem arose out of my job as a teacher, trying to teach mathematics and physics to children from 11 upwards. Over a period of five years at this, I became increasingly aware that I wasn't being as successful at this as I wished. Some pupils did well, but others seemed to have a blockage for mathematics. It was not lack of intelligence or hard work, on their side or mine. So we had a problem: a problem not confined to myself as a teacher, nor to these particular children as pupils. This was in the late 1940s: since then, awareness of this problem has become widespread.

An outcome of this was that I became increasingly interested in psychology, went back to university, and took a psychology degree. Problems of learning and teaching are psychological problems, so it was reasonable to expect that by studying psychology I would find answers to my professional problems as a teacher.

Unfortunately I didn't. Learning theory at that time was dominated by behaviourism; theories of intelligence were dominated by psychometrics. Neither of these theories (or groups of theories) was of any help in solving my professional problems as a teacher. This I had come to realize long before the end of my degree course, during which I was still teaching part-time to support myself. This kept me close to the problems of the classroom.

So now I also had a theoretical problem, namely that of finding a theory appropriate to the learning of mathematics. It turned out to be a do-it-yourself job, which is partly why it took so long. The other reason is conveyed by the well-known joke about the person who asked the way to (let us call it) Exville, and was told 'If I wanted to get to Exville, I wouldn't start from here.' I too was starting from the wrong beginnings. Behaviourist models are helpful in understanding those forms of learning which we have in common with the laboratory rat and pigeon; and it has to be admitted that for too many children, the word mathematics has become a conditioned anxiety stimulus. But the learning of mathematics with understanding exemplifies the kind of learning in which humans most differ from the lower animals: so for this we need a different kind of theoretical model. Likewise, the psychometric models of intelligence on which, as a mature student, I learnt to pass my exams, were not such as could be applied to the learning process. Measurement may tell us 'how much' intelligence a person has, but it does not tell us what it is they have this amount of. The use of a noun here tends to mislead, unless it is expanded. It is helpful to compare this with our use of the word 'memory'. When we say that someone has a good memory, we mean that this person is well able to take in information, organize it, store it, and retrieve from his large memory store just what he needs at any particular time. We are talking about a cluster of mental abilities which, collectively, are very useful.

If we continue along this line of thinking, the next question which arises is, what are these abilities which collectively comprise the functioning of human intelligence? If we can answer some of these questions, we shall be on the way to relating intelligence and learning.

Mathematics as a mental tool, and amplifier of human intelligence

All the time I was working on the psychology of learning mathematics, I was also working on the psychology of intelligent learning. Initially I did not realize this. But gradually I came to perceive mathematics as a particularly clear and concentrated example of the activity of human intelligence, and to feel a need to generalize my thinking about the learning of mathematics into a theory for intelligent learning which would be applicable to all subjects: and for teaching which would help this to take place. For it became ever more clear that mathematics was not the only subject which was badly taught and ill understood: it just showed up more sharply in mathematics.

The desire became intensified in 1973, when I moved from the University of Manchester to that of Warwick, and from a

Psychology to an Education department. Over the next five years I continued to work on this, and the outcome has been nothing less than a new model for intelligence itself.[8]

This is an ambitious undertaking. But the earlier models, based on I.Q. and its measurement, have been with us now for about seventy years; and while they may have developed much expertise in the measurement of intelligence, they tell us little or nothing about how it functions, why it is a good thing to have, and how to make the best use of whatever intelligence we possess. Until we turn our thoughts from measurement to function, the most important questions about intelligence will remain not only unanswered, but barely even asked.

Like the traveller returning to London, I now see mathematics in a new perspective: and it is this which the present book will try to communicate. Within this perspective, mathematics may now be seen, first, as a particularly powerful and concentrated example of the functioning of human intelligence; and second, as one of the most powerful and adaptable mental tools which the intelligence of man has made for its own use, collectively over the centuries. There is a close analogy between this and the use of our hands to make physical tools. We can do quite a lot with our bare hands, directly on the physical world. But we also use our hands to make a variety of tools – screwdrivers, cranes, lathes – and these greatly amplify the abilities of our hands. This is an indirect activity, but long-term it is exceedingly powerful. Likewise, mathematics is a way of using our minds which greatly increases the power of our thinking. Hence its importance in today's world of rapidly advancing science, high technology and commerce.

If this view is correct, then it is predictable that children – or, indeed, learners of any age – will not succeed in learning mathematics unless they are taught in ways which enable them to bring their intelligence, rather than rote learning, into use for their learning of mathematics. This was not, and still is not, likely to happen as long as for the majority of educational psychologists, and those who listen to them, intelligence is so closely linked with I.Q. that the two are almost synonymous. We thus return to the question: what are the activities which collectively make up the *functioning* of intelligence? We need at least some of the answers to this question before we can begin to devise learning situations which evoke these activities

– i.e., which evoke intelligent learning. So the emphasis of this book is partly theoretical, offering a new perspective for our thinking about human intelligence; and partly applied, showing how this can be embodied in classroom methods and materials. I nearly wrote '. . . partly theoretical and partly practical', which would have been to contradict myself. For many years I have been saying 'There's nothing so practical as a good theory', even before I knew that I was paraphrasing something Dewey had written in 1929.[9] But the power of theory is only potential, and it often takes years of work after a theory has been developed to put it successfully to use for the benefit of ourselves and of society. When this too has been done, the results can be spectacular, as we know from the marvels now on offer in the realm of commercial technology and modern medicine. These are at the level of the physical environment, and the physical workings of our bodies. We need power of a similar kind at a mental level, in our use of our intelligence for learning and action. The application of this power in our classrooms is still in its pioneering days, but enough progress has been made for teachers to begin putting it to work. This is the endeavour in which I am inviting readers to take part.

School mathematics and mathematics in the adult world: a false contrast

If we consider the uses of reading by adults and children, we find continuity. As adults we read for information, for entertainment, and to expand our mental horizons, among other reasons. We read to know 'how to do it', in a great variety of matters according to our needs and interests: cooking, gardening, household 'do-it-yourself', how to use our new word-processor. Sometimes we read simply to know: about life before man, about the solar system, about the lives of great men and women. This knowledge is not of any obvious practical value, but it enlarges and enriches our minds, and this we find sufficient reason in itself. And we read simply for entertainment: adventures, romances, detective stories, science fiction, or whatever our tastes may be. There is plenty of good reading for children too in all of these areas, and they enjoy and benefit from it as much as we do. These books are to be found both in and out of school. There is continuity between these two environments, and between the reasons why children learn to read at school and why it will be both useful to them, and an enrichment to their lives, when they are grown up.

Regrettably, this is not the case with mathematics, as most children experience it in school. Here they learn (incorrectly) at best that mathematics is for getting ticks or other signs of approval from teachers, for satisfying expectations of adults, for passing exams: or, in Erlwanger's memorable words, as 'a set of rules for making arcane marks on paper';[10] and at worst for avoiding reproof or other punishment, for avoiding being made to feel stupid, or to appear stupid in front of their fellows. These are not the reasons why mathematics is of such importance in the adult world. Let us take a closer look at what these are.

Earlier, I suggested that mathematics could be seen as a particularly powerful and concentrated example of the functioning of human intelligence; and also as one of the most powerful and adaptable mental tools which the intelligence of man has made for its own use, collectively over the centuries. In the latter aspect, it acts as an amplifier of our intelligence. Here are some examples.

When we travel by air on holiday or business, we may be out of sight of land for much of the time, either above cloud or over the ocean. The navigator, by his understanding of the mathematics of navigation, brings us exactly to our destination. If we should be blown off course, or diverted to a different airport, from the same knowledge base he would work out a revised course. Both in making and using these plans he relies on sophisticated equipment, largely electronic. The design of this equipment, and its use, are based on theory which is formulated largely in mathematical terms. The maps which the navigator uses are based on the concept of proportionality, and so also are the scale drawings which were used in the design and construction of the aircraft itself. The extra power which mathematics gives to our thinking is indispensable in all these cases, and likewise in so many other cases that it is hard to see how the science and technology of today could exist or function without it.

The concepts and language of mathematics are also of social

and economic importance, in that they provide a basis for the co-operation, and exchange of goods and services, on which our present technological cultures depend. Even at a descriptive level, it is often only by the use of the measurement function of mathematics that we can give descriptions of physical objects and events which are exact enough for everyone's contribution to fit together. Manufacturers couldn't make nuts to fit bolts, shoes to fit feet, tyres to fit wheels, without this use of mathematics. Still less so, when describing invisible quantities such as the resistance of a wire, the impedance of a coil, the capacity of a condenser, by which the components of an electronic apparatus are fitted together.

Many of these objects are bought and sold across national boundaries, which involves exchange of currencies. This too is based on the mathematics of proportionality, as well as simpler operations such as addition (to the account of the seller) and subtraction (from the account of the buyer). Without international agreement about the mathematics involved, commerce on this scale would be impossible.

These two uses of mathematics are particular cases of two of the major uses of human intelligence in general: as a mental tool, and for co-operation. These uses are also deeply rooted in our nature, since *homo sapiens* has evolved, and has reached its dominant position on this planet, as a tool-using species which succeeds in the competition for survival by co-operation with each other. Nor is utility the only reason for learning mathematics. It has an aesthetic quality, and it also exemplifies an aspect of human creativity, by which our mental horizons are expanded in ways which complement those already described in our discussion of reading.

If the reasons why mathematics is so important in the adult world are of these three kinds, then surely we should try to provide experiences of the same kinds for children whereby they can experience the power and enjoyment of mathematics in their present realities, rather than assure them 'that this will be useful to you when you grow up.' One of the main purposes of the present book is to suggest how this can be done.

Summary

1 After more than twenty years of effort to improve mathematical education, there appears to have been little improvement. The problem is widespread. Unless we can identify at least some of the reasons why mathematics is still a problem subject for many, there is no reason to suppose that future efforts will be more successful than those of the past.

2 The problem will not be solved from a viewpoint which is confined to mathematics itself, and relies on changes of content alone. A wider perspective is needed.

3 Mathematics may be seen as a particularly powerful and concentrated example of the functioning of human intelligence. Also as a powerful and adaptable mental tool, and amplifier of human intelligence. If this view is accepted, it follows that learners of any age will not succeed at mathematics unless they are taught in ways which enable them to bring their intelligence, rather than rote learning, into use for their learning of mathematics. To do this we need to understand more about how intelligence functions. Measures of intelligence do not tell us this.

4 We also need to teach mathematics in ways which have continuity between school and the outside world. This is already the case with reading, but with mathematics there is a false contrast.

Suggested activities for readers

1 With a group of colleagues, or any other group for which it seems appropriate, try the following. Ask if they would be willing to take part in a simple experiment: those who prefer may abstain.

   Ask them to take their minds back to their time at school, and think which was the subject which for them gave most problems: which they didn't like, or found hard to understand, or which made them afraid that they would be made to look stupid in front of their classmates. After that, ask for a show of hands to find out which were the problem subjects. History? Geography? English? French? German? Mathematics? Science? Drama . . .? The group may like to discuss the results of this mini-survey.

2 Look back to the section starting on p. 27: 'School mathematics and mathematics in the adult world: a false contrast'. Make your own list of ways in which mathematics increases our powers of thinking and action in the adult world. These may be grouped under three headings: the physical environment (e.g. science and technology); social, including commercial; and creativity. I have not yet given examples in the third group, but shall do so later. It is mentioned here only because some of your own examples may come into this category. Note that the groups are not mutually exclusive: some examples come into two, or even three, of these groups.

2

Intelligence and understanding

Habit learning *vs* intelligent learning

This chapter is about the power which comes with understanding, and the ways in which we can use our intelligence to gain this power. In Chapter 1, intelligence was described as a cluster of mental abilities which, together, are very useful. Here we shall begin to examine in greater detail what these abilities are. The first of these is an ability to learn in a special way, which can most clearly be distinguished by contrasting it with habit learning.

Suppose that we need to learn someone's telephone number. This is a matter of rote memorizing. Suppose now that to pass some examination, perhaps one necessary to qualify as a secretary, we were required to memorize several long lists of telephone numbers. This task would arouse no interest, and give us no pleasure. The work would be regarded as boring and difficult, and we would only do it because we had to. One of the things which makes this task difficult is the fact that once we have memorized one telephone number, this knowledge is of little use in helping to memorize the next. The more we try to learn, the greater the memory load, and the harder the task becomes.

In contrast, suppose that for some other reason we were asked to learn the following sequence of numbers:

4 7 10 13 16 19 22 . . . (a hundred of these in all)

This has a pattern, and once we had seen the pattern, we would not try to memorize all the numbers. We would learn just the first number, four, and the pattern: the numbers increase by three each time. This provides a generating structure from which the whole sequence can be derived. In so doing, we would be using our minds in a different way. We would be using intelligent learning.

Also in contrast to habit learning, knowledge of this second kind is highly adaptable. For example, if asked what would be the hundredth number, or the ninety-ninth, we could work this out from the pattern. And we would not need to restrict ourselves to a hundred numbers. Make the list twice as long, and the memory load is no greater. Make it as long as we choose – the task of constructing the later numbers in the sequence becomes a little harder, but not greatly so. This is the kind of extra power we get from intelligent learning.

Habit learning has been extensively studied by the behaviourist school of psychologists, mainly with animals. A well-known textbook example is provided by the Skinner box. A hungry rat is put in a cage, in which there is a bar sticking out horizontally from one side. In the course of its movements around the cage, the rat happens to press the bar, and a morsel of food is released into the cage. Eating the food reduces hunger, and each time this happens, the association between the stimulus situation (being in the cage, hungry) and bar-pressing is reinforced. Gradually this builds up into a habit.

In this kind of learning, certain actions are reinforced as a result of their outcomes, so learning *follows* action. And what is learnt *is* action: the cognitive element is small. Rote learning, as in the telephone numbers example, is verbal habit learning.

Once learnt, habits tend to be very persistent: they have low adaptability. If our telephone number is changed, we can't erase the old number from our minds the way we do from our desk pad. The old number persists, and gets in the way of the new one.

In contrast, the main feature of intelligent learning is adaptability. By this, I mean that for a given goal, we can find a variety of different ways of achieving it to suit a variety of different situations.

If we are thirsty and want a drink of water, at home we probably go to the kitchen and turn on the tap. In a café, we ask a waitress. In camp, we find a clear stream, or a spring. As a child when on holiday, I went to the yard and worked a pump handle. Several winters ago when our pipes froze, our breakfast coffee was made with melted snow. Different environments, different plans of action, all directed towards the same goal: relief of thirst.

At the level of habit learning, there is some justification for the behaviourist view that our behaviour is shaped by the environment. In sharp contrast, the present model for intelligent learning asserts that we shape our own behaviour, to achieve the same goals in different environments. Behaviour is goal-directed, using flexible plans of action which can be constructed in advance of action, and modified in the light of action. These plans enable us to achieve goals of our own choosing, in a wide variety of situations. What is more, we can devise several plans, and choose the best, before putting this plan into action. Intelligent learning often *precedes* action. And action is used not only for achieving goals, but for testing hypotheses. Each plan is based on knowledge of the environment; and building up this knowledge is a major function of intelligence. Action is not a response to an external stimulus, but directed towards whatever goal an individual has in his own mind. The cognitive element is great, and as a result, so is the variety of available plans. *Knowledge gives adaptability.*

One of the greatest mistakes of the behaviourists was to think that habit learning is the only kind. We must not make the opposite mistake, of insisting that intelligent learning is the only kind. We need both. Habit learning, with rote learning as a special case, can be useful and necessary even in mathematics. It is by habit learning that children learn the spoken words for the number-concepts one, two, three, four, five, . . .; and the written symbols 1, 2, 3, 4, 5, . . . which mean the same. It is by habit learning that we know that π = 3.14159. . . . π *can* be derived from a particular kind of series, but this is not the best way for everyday use. What matters is to use the right kind for each particular requirement, and the right combination for the subject overall.

Mathematics requires mainly intelligent learning. Spelling English words needs a different combination. Consider these words:

COW, NOW, VOW, and BOW (respectfully)
       BOW (and arrow)
       BOUGH (on a tree)
       BOUGHT
       TROUGH
       ENOUGH

In the top line, spelling and pronunciation are regular. Reading down the right-hand column, however, we have different pronunciations with the same spelling, and different spellings with the same pronunciation. So we need to use intelligent learning when spelling and pronunciation are regular, and habit learning (in this case we would call it rote memorizing) when spelling and pronunciation are irregular.

Because English spelling contains much irregularity, this area of learning requires a greater proportion of habit learning. Mathematics is a highly regular subject, so learning maths requires a high proportion of intelligent learning. My own estimate is about 95 per cent intelligent learning, 5 per cent habit learning. This is, unfortunately, not how it is learnt by a large number of children, for whom learning mathematics consists of memorizing a collection of rules without reasons.

Unfortunately, it is all too easy for this to happen, since if the result is correct it is hard to tell whether this is based on rote-learning or comprehension. A rule gives quick results, and an able and willing child can memorize so many rules that the lack of understanding does not show immediately. But the time comes when this approach fails, for two reasons. First, what has been learnt in this way is (as has already been pointed out) of no help in subsequent learning. So as the mathematical content increases, the amount to be memorized becomes an impossible burden on the memory. And second, these rules only work for a limited range of problems. They cannot be adapted by the learner to related problems based on the same mathematical ideas, since with habit learning these ideas are absent. So the child comes to grief in his mathematical progress, with loss of confidence and self-esteem.

We can save the children we teach from this fate if we know how. Intelligent teaching involves knowing which kind of learning to get children to use for different kinds of task, and how to get them to use it. We are much better at the latter in the case of habit learning, which may be one of the reasons children have less difficulty in learning to spell than to do mathematics.

Goal-directed action

As has been emphasized, there is a sharp contrast between the actions which result from using our intelligence, and those which are stimulus-determined and controlled by habit or instinct. In the former case we can choose our own aims, purposes, goals – these all mean much the same, but mostly I shall use the word 'goals' since it is more general – and our intelligence helps us to achieve these by a variety of plans according to different circumstances. To the relation between these three, goal-directed action, plans of action for achieving our goals, and intelligence, we now direct our attention.

This emphasis on action as being goal-directed, rather than stimulus-determined, allows us to borrow from cybernetics the important idea of a *director system*. This is a kind of apparatus, physical or mental, which enables us to direct our actions so as to achieve our chosen goal in a variety of circumstances. The features of a director system by which it is able to do this are described in detail elsewhere.[1] For our present purposes, one of the most important of these is a *plan of action* which determines what we do, at each stage from starting point to the time when our goal is achieved. Here is one which I tried to use, a while ago. My starting point was a school in which I had been working for the first time. I had been piloted there by following someone else's car, but we were now going our separate ways. So my friend told me how to get to highway A40: once there, I knew my way home. This was the plan of action I was given.

LEFT, RIGHT, HALF-LEFT, STRAIGHT ON, LEFT, RIGHT

It is easy to guess what happened. I was soon quite lost, and it took me a long time to get home that day.

A plan of this kind is closely tied to action. And if one of the actions is wrong, it is likely to throw out all which follow. In this case, once one gets off the right path, one does not know how to get back on. In mathematics, a single mistake makes all the subsequent working wrong. One probably does not even know where one went wrong. The cognitive element is low. This is the kind of plan of action which is provided by habit learning, and a director system which has only these available is of low adaptability.

Cognitive maps, knowledge structures, mental models, and schemas

For my next visit, I made sure that I had a street map with me. Figure 2.1 gives a simplified extract from it.

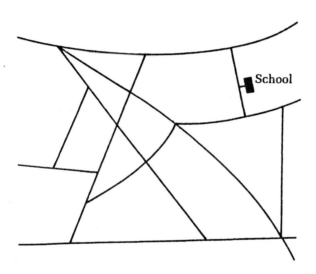

Figure 2.1

This has a number of advantages. First, I could find out where I had gone wrong.

Figure 2.2 shows the plan I was trying to use, but now not

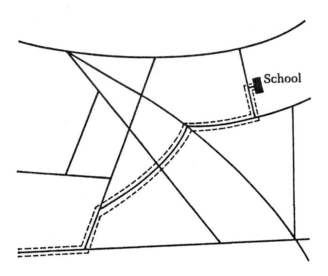

School

Figure 2.2

in isolation but in relation to the road network. From this it became clear that I had not counted the left turn at the school gate as one of the left turns to be taken: so at what should have been my first right turn, I took another left, and so was heading in the opposite direction to the correct one. But with this map, even if I did go wrong, all I had to do was to find where I was by looking at a street sign, locate this on the map, and I could then make a new plan of action to take me where I wanted. The advantage goes beyond this. Given any starting location, and any goal location, from the map one can make a plan to take one from one to the other provided only that they are both on the map. One could, for example, make a plan to take one to a post office, then a newsagent, then a coffee shop, and finally back onto the road home. The cognitive element is high, and so also is the adaptability of one's actions.

This example generalizes nicely into a number of key

concepts for intelligent learning. Using as a transitional metaphor, Tolman's useful idea of a *cognitive map*, we can see it as a particular case of a *knowledge structure*. A street map represents knowledge at a concrete level, about things which we can directly see and touch. A more general term, used by psychologists to include more abstract kinds of knowledge, is *schema*.

A model is a simplified representation of something else, and we can have mental models as well as physical. We have mental models of the neighbourhood around our home, of the place where we work, and other regions, which we use in the same way as that described in the example. We do this so habitually that it takes a situation where we are without one to bring home to us the importance of these mental models. The street map on paper provided a quick way of acquiring a mental model of a new district. Someone who could not read a map, i.e. who could not make a mental model from the marks on paper, would not have been able to use it to make plans for action. This kind of mental model is a cognitive map. Those of a more abstract kind will be discussed further in the section about theories.

The meanings of the terms cognitive map, knowledge structure, mental model, theory, and schema, are very alike. The term schema is the most general, and includes all the others; but the other terms are also useful. It is sometimes easier to think at the less abstract level of examples such as the street map, and the term 'cognitive map' allows us to do this while keeping in mind the more general idea. The other three terms enable us to centre on the uses of these particular kinds of schema.

Intelligent learning

If these schemas (including cognitive maps, knowledge structures, mental models) are so important for achieving our goals, how do we acquire them? We are not born with them. The instinctual behaviours which are genetically inherited are closely tied to action, and are even less adaptable than habits. Schemas have to be acquired by learning. So now we need to build on to our model of what is happening in our minds

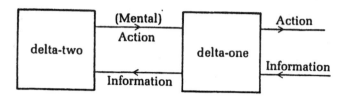

Figure 2.3

something to help us grasp what goes on at two levels, that of action and also that of learning.

For this we need two director systems, which I have called delta-one and delta-two: D stands for any kind of director system, including instincts and habits, with which we are not here concerned; and Greek D for those which are intelligent.

Delta-one is a director system whose function is to enable us to achieve our goals in relation to the physical environment. Delta-two is a second-order director system which acts on delta-one. Its function is to take delta-one to states in which delta-one can do its job more successfully. This is one of the meanings of learning – increasing our ability to do what we want: in more technical language, our ability to achieve our goals. It does this in a way which is indirect, but much more adaptable, as we have seen. It is also much more economical. In the street-map example, we can quantify this. If in Figure 2.1 we count each road junction, and each stretch of road between two junctions, as a single location, the number of these is 49. From this it can be calculated that the number of plans required to go from any one of these as starting position to any other location as goal is 2352. To remember all of these plans separately would impose an almost impossible burden on the memory. But it is learning of this kind which children are trying to achieve when they are taught in ways which do not help them to build structured knowledge. In contrast, each and every one of these plans can be constructed, if and when needed, from the unified knowledge structure represented by the map. It is learning of this kind with which intelligence is particularly concerned; and though its function is one step removed from action, it makes action more likely to succeed because each plan is constructed for each particular task.

Intelligence thus contributes to adaptability in two ways.

1 By the construction of schemas – not just one, but a large number, for all the different kinds of job that delta-one does.
2 By constructing from these schemas particular plans appropriate to different initial states and goal states. These plans can then form the basis of goal-directed action as already outlined.

This way of using our minds is not only more efficient: it is more pleasurable for the learner. And witnessing this enjoyment is one of the rewards one experiences when teaching children to use their intelligence for learning mathematics.

What is understanding, and why does it matter?

In 1971 I wrote 'What is understanding, and by what means can we help to bring it about? We certainly think we know whether we understand something or not; and most of us have a fairly deep-rooted belief that it matters. But just what happens when we understand, that does not happen when we don't, most of us have no idea.'[2] And I went on to suggest that until we did, we would not be in a good position to bring about understanding in others. I wrote from experience, for it was as a teacher of mathematics in school that my interest in these problems first arose. Later in the the same publication I offered an answer to this question. 'To understand something means to assimilate it into an appropriate schema.'[3] In the light of the previous section, we can take this thinking two steps further. We can now explain the greater power of action which is made available by understanding, and we can also relate this to the feelings which accompany non-understanding and understanding.

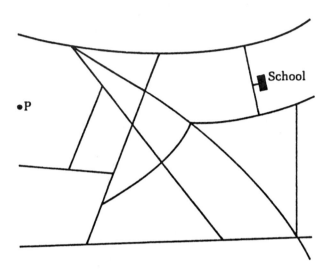

School

●P

Figure 2.4

Our cognitive maps, or schemas, are, as we have seen, the sources from which delta-two constructs plans of action for use by delta-one. But suppose now that we encounter an experience which we cannot connect to any of our existing schemas (Figure 2.4).

Delta-two cannot make any plan which includes point P (that is to say, what this point represents). If, as in the original example, this represents a road map, then we are literally lost here. If it represents a cognitive map or schema, we are mentally 'lost'. The metaphor is a close one: we do not know what to do in order to achieve any goal at all. And this, in general terms, is our state of mind when confronted with some object, experience, situation, or idea which we do not understand.

The achievement of understanding, as represented in Figure 2.5, makes connections with an existing schema. We are now

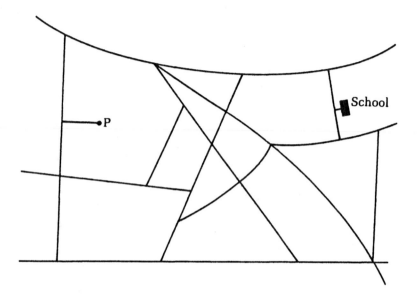

Figure 2.5

able to cope with the new situation, since our delta-two can once more make plans if and as needed. Metaphorically, and in some cases literally, we know where we are, and so we can find a way to where we want to arrive. This change of mental state gives us a degree of control over the situation which we did not have before, and is signalled emotionally by a change from insecurity to confidence.

Habit learning and teacher-dependence *vs* understanding and confidence

For habit learning, we are largely dependent on outside events. The rat is given the food if it presses the lever. In schools, we provide these events by awarding symbolic rewards or punishments such as ticks and crosses. In mathematics, we also have to explain to the children how to get these ticks and avoid the crosses. Not having the necessary mathematical schemas, they cannot find out for themselves.

In the case of intelligent learning, the achievement of understanding is itself rewarding, as may be seen from children's faces. I believe that it is part of our job as teachers to provide learning situations by which children can achieve understanding largely by their own endeavours. Exposition by a teacher still has its importance; but it has a different function, that of helping children's efforts to understand for themselves. Learners who have experienced the satisfaction which results from understanding are likely to make these efforts.

The map analogy will stand us in good stead once again. When away from home, we may need to ask for help in finding our way. The question 'How do I get to . . .?' usually evokes one kind of help, directions of the 'what to do' kind. Like the 'left, left, . . .' example, it is hard to remember anything longer than a short list, and if one goes astray one is dependent on further help. But if one asks 'Please could you show me where I am on this map?', the resulting information puts one in the position of being more able to help oneself thereafter. The latter, of course, usually depends on the enquirer having already acquired a map, or being given one. When on holiday last summer, I asked at a visitors' information centre how to get to our hotel. In response I was given a little map on which I was shown 'This is where you are now. Here is your hotel. So (drawing on the map) you turn right out of the car park, over the bridge, . . .'. As well as enabling us to find our hotel, this combination enabled us to find our way around for the rest of our stay. It would be hard to improve on this as a demonstration of how to help those in unfamiliar territory. A cognitive map of a more abstract kind takes longer to communicate, but the principle remains entirely the same.

Habit learning and intelligent learning thus develop two different kinds of learner-teacher relationship and two states of mind. Habit learning keeps the learner dependent on being told what to do in every new situation, with little confidence in his own ability to cope if left on his own. Intelligent learning develops the learner's confidence in his own ability to deal with any situation which can be understood in relation to his existing knowledge, and encourages perception of the teacher as someone who can help him to increase this knowledge, and thereby his power of understanding.

What are theories, and why do we need them?

Even at an everyday level, much of what we do depends on our having mental models of our environment. Suppose that we want a drink of water. If there is a jug of water in sight, there may seem to be no problem. But even in this simple case, we need to be aware of properties beyond those immediately visible, such as pourability. If there is no water in sight, then we need to have a mental model of the building we are in. At home, this will include a kitchen with a cold water tap. If we are working away from home, the model will be a different one, within which is represented a cloakroom, and within the cloakroom washbasins with cold water taps. This model of the building may usefully also include a room where the secretaries work, another room where we can use a photo-copier, and beyond this other useful locations such as a car park, somewhere to eat. Without such a model, we cannot direct our steps to places where we can satisfy our needs. So even at the simplest level, and although we learn and use them with hardly a thought, these mental models are indispensable to us. They take us beyond dependence on what we can see and hear at any present time.

Slightly more advanced are models at a common-sense level. These further increase our power to understand, predict, and control events in the physical world. They relate for the most part to objects and events which are accessible to our senses, and we use them still in much the same ways as mankind has done before us for thousands of years. Wood floats, so it is good for making boats. Iron sinks, so nobody would for a moment consider making an iron boat unless he had a more powerful mental model: in this case, the principle of Archimedes. This operates beyond a common-sense level: it is an example of a theory.

The distinction between a theory and a common-sense mental model is one of degree rather than of kind: namely, its degree of abstractness and generality. When as children we have our first bicycles, we may acquire a common-sense model in which turning the pedals makes the back wheel go round, and this pushes us forward. If we begin to see how the chain-drive converts the slower rotations of the pedals into faster rotations of the rear wheel, our mental model is changing in the direction of a theory. If when we are older we relate this to a general model of velocity ratios, depending on the ratio of the numbers of the cogs in the two gear wheels, we now have a theory, albeit a fairly simple one. Further development of this theory enables us to understand how a multi-speed gear works. The engineer who designed this gear used the same theory, which also relates velocity ratios with mechanical advantage – how hard we have to push on the pedals, and so which gears are best for downhill and level riding, and which for moderate or steep hills. We may also know that a bicycle wheel by itself tends to keep upright so long as it is rolling along; but much more advanced knowledge is required before this can be explained in terms of a theory.

Theories are both more powerful and more general than common-sense models. In the natural sciences, some of this generality often comes from their use of mathematical models, which are themselves notable for their generality. The mathematical model for velocity ratio and mechanical advantage can be used to design gearboxes for motor cars, clocks and watches (of the old kind), mixing machines for the kitchen, winches, lathes. The mathematical theory of spinning tops and flywheels can be used for gyro-compasses and auto-pilots.

Another feature of a theory is that it sometimes predicts events which are contrary to common sense. The iron ship which floats is one example. If we hold a rotating bicycle wheel by the hub, and try to change the plane of rotation, the wheel not only resists our efforts but tries to twist in quite an unexpected direction. Someone who understands the mathematical theory of spinning tops and gyroscopes can predict this. As a result their thinking is, in this context, more powerful than that of most of us.

An essential feature of a theory is that it helps us to understand the invisible causes which lie beyond the visible effects. And the more remote from what is accessible to our senses are these hidden causes, the more we need a theory before we can deal adequately with the situation.

When children fall and bruise themselves we do not normally need a theory to deal with the situation. Common sense is enough. But when a little boy is very ill after a fall from which a normal child would take no harm, then we need to know about the possibility that he has haemophilia. The explanation of this requires a mental model far beyond common sense. It is based on theories of genetics, bio-chemistry, and physiology.

A person who intervenes in the workings of the human body needs a mental model beyond common sense, if he is to do more good than harm. (Medieval doctors often did more harm than good.) And if as teachers we intervene in the mental processes of a growing child, which are even more inaccessible to our senses, the same applies.

Summary

1 Intelligence has already been described as a cluster of related mental abilities, which together are very useful. Among these is the ability to learn in a way which is qualitatively different from habit learning.

2 Intelligent learning consists, not in the memorizing of a collection of rules, but in the building up of knowledge structures from which a great variety of plans of action can be derived as and when required. Constructing these plans from existing knowledge is another function of intelligence.

3 This is a much more economical form of learning, since the number of plans which can be derived from the same knowledge structure is enormously greater than the number of rules which can be memorized separately.

4 Intelligent learning is more adaptable, since plans can be constructed to meet circumstances for which a rule has not yet been devised.

5 It is also more powerful, since plans are individually made to fit the given situation, and are thus likely to be more effective.

6 The learning of most subjects requires a combination of intelligent learning and habit learning. The proportion varies between subjects. For mathematics, the proportion may be estimated as 95 per cent intelligent learning,

5 per cent habit learning.

7 The general term 'schema' includes knowledge structures, and also cognitive maps and mental models.

8 In the present theory of intelligence, understanding is conceived as relating new experiences or ideas to an existing schema. Until this has been achieved, we are unable to plan how to achieve our goals in any situation which involves these experiences or ideas. We feel lost, and unable to cope. Understanding extends our powers of adaptation to the new situation: so we are correct in our intuitive feeling that understanding is important to us.

9 Habit learning develops a learner's dependence on a teacher to continue the supply of rules for each new kind of situation. Intelligent learning develops a learner's confidence in his own abilities to cope with new situations, and perception of his teacher as someone who can help him to increase his own understanding.

10 Theories are mental models which are more abstract and general than common-sense ones. They increase our power to understand the invisible causes behind visible events. If, as teachers, we intervene in the mental processes of a growing child, without an appropriate theory we may do more harm than good.

Suggested activities for readers

1 Reflect on the way you yourself learnt mathematics at school. How much of this did you learn by the use of your intelligence, i.e. with understanding, and how much consisted of memorizing rules? Were you encouraged to ask questions if there was something you did not understand?

2 Choose one or more other subjects which you have learnt, not necessarily academic. Within the same subject area, identify some parts for which habit learning would be the most effective kind, and others for which intelligent learning should be used. Compare the results of your own analysis with the ways in which you were taught.

3

The formation of mathematical concepts

The special demands of mathematics

The mathematician Henri Poincaré, in his essay 'Mathematical creation', wrote:

> A first fact should surprise us, or rather would surprise us if we were not so used to it. How does it happen that there are people who do not understand mathematics?[1]

It is interesting to find this question asked nearly a hundred years ago, by a famous mathematician rather than a mathematics educator. With a different emphasis, it is the same question as we began with, and it is a good question. People do not seem to have this difficulty in understanding history, or geography, or in learning to speak a foreign language. If they make the necessary efforts at any of these, there is every likelihood that they will succeed. But people can work very hard at mathematics with little or no understanding at the end of it: and 'people' here for the most part means children, since a majority of adults have given it up as a bad job. The minority who have succeeded in understanding mathematics find it hard to understand the problems of those who have failed. So what is different about mathematics? Does it require special aptitudes which are found in only a few?

Research evidence suggests that this is not the case, except perhaps for high-flying specialist mathematicians.[2] In its early stages, mathematical thinking is not essentially different from some of the ways in which we use our intelligence in everyday life. But for many children, this continuity between mathematics and the everyday use of their intelligence is never established. And if it is not, then from the very beginning mathematics is something apart. This is another aspect of the false distinction between school mathematics and the mathematics of the world outside school which was discussed in Chapter 1.

So this is part of the answer. Following on from this, in Chapter 2 the nature of intelligence itself was considered in more detail, and it was suggested that if children do not use intelligent learning rather than habit learning for their mathematics from the very beginning, then long-term they are likely to fail.

However, though mathematics does not need different mental abilities from those which characterize intelligence, the nature of the subject requires that these abilities are used in special ways. It also calls for teaching which makes these special ways possible. What these ways are, and what it is about mathematics which demands them, will be explored in this chapter and the next.

The abstract nature of mathematics

Mathematics is much more abstract than any of the other subjects which children are taught at the same age, and this leads to special difficulties of communication. It is instructive to experience this difficulty at one's own level of thinking. Here, by way of illustration, are three pairs of statements.

1 (a) My pocket knife will sink if I drop it in the river. A piece of wood will float.
  (b) Trains for London leave Coventry at 6 and 36 minutes past each hour.

Both of these are understandable by an average seven-year-old child. The second is a little harder than the first.

2 (a) Iron sinks because its density is greater than that of water. A hot air balloon rises because the density of hot air is less than that of cold air.
  (b) The reason why high voltage electricity is used for powering electric trains is that a smaller current is

needed to give the same power, and this results in smaller losses in transmission between the power station and the locomotive.

A majority of readers are likely to understand the first of these statements, and also the second in general terms. A fuller understanding of the second requires a little knowledge of electrical theory. It may well be that a little time for thought is required, also. They are not as easy as the first two.

3 (a) The amount of information, being the negative logarithm of a quantity which we may consider as a probability, is essentially a negative entropy.[3]

(b) Let V be a finite dimensional vector space over the field F. The number of elements in a basis of V is the dimension of V.[4]

Those who can understand the last pair of statements (they are from advanced texts on cybernetics and geometry, respectively) are few. Clearly these statements increase in difficulty, from the first pair to the third. But where does the difficulty lie? The importance of this question is that the difficulty which the reader has just experienced is the same kind of difficulty which so many children encounter in trying to understand mathematics at the levels presented to them. It has something to do with the statements being progressively more abstract: but just what do we mean by 'more abstract'? We know what we mean by 'more heavy' or 'more expensive', but do we know what is 'more abstract'? Indeed, what do we mean by 'abstract'? Even if we think we know at an intuitive level, can we put this knowledge clearly into words? We need to have an explicit and analytic understanding of these ideas before we can put them to work in our teaching, and thereby begin to make it easier for our pupils to learn with understanding.

The necessity of conceptual learning

As a beginning, I suggest that we should be more surprised than we are that we can recognize the same person on different occasions. The light may be different, we may see them at a different angle, they may be paler if it is cold, their expression may be different. The retinal image is different on every occasion. But beyond these differences we perceive something in common, and it is this which enables us to know that it is the same person. In the same kind of way, we can recognize the same person's voice, whatever words they are speaking.

This exemplifies, in everyday experience, an ability which is a key feature at all levels of learning. The present experiences from which (sometimes) we learn become part of our past, and will never again be encountered in exactly the same form. But the situations in which we need to apply what we have learned lie in the future as it becomes our present; or as, by anticipation, we bring the future into our present thinking and planning. From this it follows that if our mental models are to be of any use to us, they must represent, not singletons from among the infinite variety of actual events, but common properties of past experiences which we are able to recognize on future occasions.

Abstraction and the process of concept formation

A mental representation of these common properties is how, for many years now, I have described a concept; and for this process of concept formation I use the term 'abstraction'. Concepts represent, not isolated experiences, but regularities abstracted from these. It is only because, and to the extent that, our environment is orderly and not capricious that learning of any kind is possible. A major feature of intelligent learning is the discovery of these regularities, and the organizing of them into conceptual structures which are themselves orderly. In this chapter, we shall consider the first of these processes: the formation of concepts, and in particular of mathematical concepts. In the next chapter we shall examine how these are built up into conceptual structures.

To begin with, let us consider how we might try to communicate the meaning of a simple everyday word to a person who has been blind from birth, but who has recently been given sight by a corneal graft. Such a person is entering into what is for him a totally new field of experience, so his situation is not unlike that of a child learning mathematics for the first time. He asks 'What does "red" mean?'

Intuitively, we would know that a verbal definition such as 'Red is the colour we experience from light in the region of 0.6 microns' would be useless to him. Instead we might point and say, 'These are red socks. This is a red diary. That tulip is red.' And so on. In this way, though we could not tell him, we could arrange for him to find out the meaning for himself.

Let us now verbalize our intuitive awareness of the right approach, in this particular example, in the light of the description of the process of concept formation which has just been given. The purpose of doing so will be that already stated: to achieve an explicit and analytic understanding, which can be generalized to other appropriate situations, and which will help us to distinguish which are appropriate situations and which are not.

The meaning of a word is the concept associated with that word. This concept is not the word itself, so let us distinguish between them by using 'red' for the word and *red* (without quotes) for the concept. (Italic type face, though not essential for this distinction, is useful to distinguish particular concepts under discussion.) The meaning of 'red', i.e. the concept *red*, is an awareness of something in common between the experiences he has just had. (Not between the objects themselves, but between his own visual experiences in looking at them.) Without these or similar experiences, it would not have been possible for him to form the concept. By arranging for him to have these experiences, we make it possible for him to form the concept. Possible, and in this case probable: but not certain. Concept formation has to happen in the learner's own mind, and we cannot do it for him. What we can do, as teachers, is greatly to help along the natural learning processes, if we know enough about these.

On further reflection we can see that in this example, two kinds of learning are happening simultaneously, conceptual and associative. As was said earlier, the meaning of the word 'red' is its attached concept. From the visual set of experiences, our subject abstracts the concept *red*. From the words we use while indicating these, 'red socks', 'red diary', 'that tulip is red', he abstracts what these descriptions have in common: the word 'red'. And by associative learning, he attaches the concept to the word.

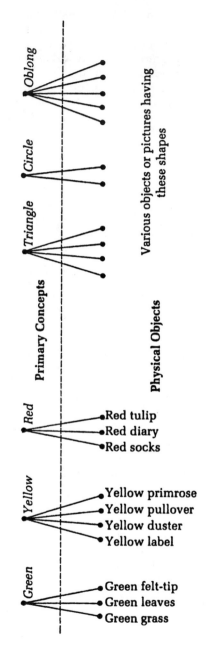

Figure 3.1

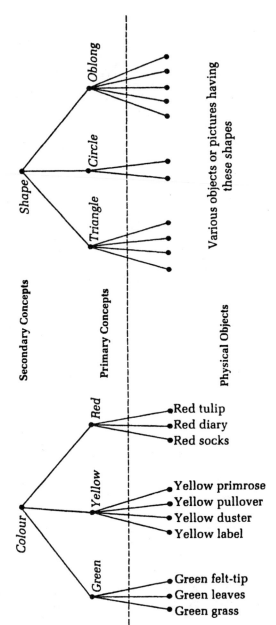

Figure 3.2

Successive abstraction: primary and secondary concepts

Not all concepts can be conveyed in this way. Suppose that our subject has asked for the meaning of 'colour'. Our intuition would in this case tell us that it would be no good trying to communicate this by pointing. Instead, we would use words, and say something like: 'green, yellow, red . . . these are all colours.' By again analysing our intuition, we can arrive at two new and important ideas relative to concepts.

Primary and secondary concepts

Figure 3.1 illustrates the nature of primary concepts. Primary concepts are those which are derived directly from sensory experiences. In the above figure, *green, yellow, red* and *triangle, circle, oblong* are primary concepts. Other examples of primary concepts are *hot, cold, heavy, smooth, sweet, lavender* (the smell).

Figure 3.2 illustrates the difference between primary and secondary concepts. *Colour* is a secondary concept, which is formed when we realize what the concepts *green, yellow, red* etc. have in common. When we have this concept, we can also recognize that *blue* is a colour, and *square* is not. Secondary concepts thus depend on other concepts, and can only be formed if the person already has these concepts, which may be primary concepts, or themselves other secondary concepts.

We see from figure 3.3 that *attribute* is also a secondary concept, in this case derived from other secondary concepts.

Lower- and higher-order concepts

When we centre our attention on the common property of a set of objects (which may be mental objects), and ignore for the time being their individual differences, we are 'pulling out', or abstracting this common property. The result of this mental activity is what we call a concept. However, formation of the concept *attribute* involves more stages of abstraction than the concepts *colour, shape*. So now we have a meaning for 'more abstract': *attribute* is a more abstract concept than *colour* and

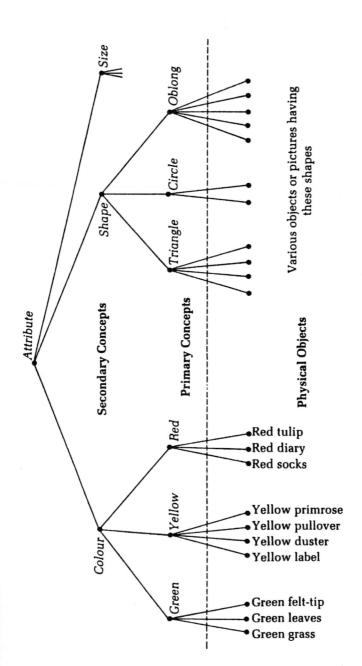

Figure 3.3

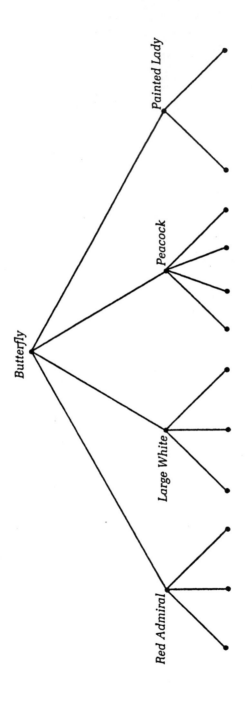

Figure 3.4

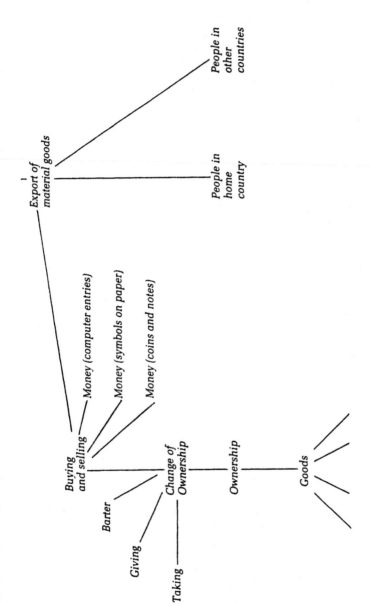

Figure 3.5

shape, and similarly *colour* is a more abstract concept than *green, yellow, red*. These concepts thus form a hierarchy, in which the terms 'higher-order' and 'lower-order' describe the same relationships as 'more abstract' and 'less abstract'. These also mean further away from, or nearer to, direct sensory experience.

Everyday concepts and mathematical concepts

We have seen that all intelligent learning involves abstracting from a number of examples something which they have in common, and that the mental object which results is what we mean by a concept. However, between different subjects there are differences in the availability of examples. Let us take two contrasting areas of knowledge: butterflies and invisible exports.

Examples of concepts such as *butterfly*, and of particular varieties such as *peacock, painted lady*, are readily available in the outside world (at the right time of year), and children often become remarkably knowledgeable in areas of this kind with little or no teaching beyond, say, a book from which to get the names for attaching to the concepts. The concept *butterfly* is itself a primary concept, and children are likely to learn this first, and subsequently to differentiate between varieties, as shown in Figure 3.4.

But if someone asks 'What is an invisible export?', the examples from which this concept may be abstracted are not visible in the environment. This is a high-order secondary concept, for which the contributors are other concepts, such as the *export of material goods, money which is not coin or note* but a matter of accountancy, *insurance, tourism, banking*. These are also very abstract, being themselves dependent on other lower-order concepts. Figure 3.5 gives some of the lower-order concepts required for just *export of material goods*.

These two contrasting examples of schemas are at opposite ends of a continuum. Those at the 'butterfly' end of the continuum contain only primary concepts and concepts of a low order of abstraction, and their interdependence is not great. Those at the 'invisible export' end of the continuum contain few or no primary concepts, and many concepts of a high order of abstraction.

The interdependence between the individual concepts is much greater in subjects of the second kind. In the butterfly schema, the concept *Painted Lady* does not depend on the concept *Red Admiral*, and each of these could be replaced by another variety without affecting one's overall understanding of butterflies. And small though it is as here shown, this schema is sufficient for forming the concept *butterfly*, so that if someone having this schema asks 'What is a fritillary?' they will understand when told that it is a kind of butterfly. But in the invisible export schema, there is hardly a single concept which is not necessary for understanding of those above it in the hierarchy. And yet Figure 3.5 is incomplete: it still shows only one of the hierarchies involved. Those required for the concepts *banking, insurance, tourism*, are also needed for the concept *invisible export*, and each of these similarly involves concepts of increasing levels of abstraction.

These two examples illustrate one of the major differences between mathematics and most of the other subjects which children learn at primary school; and indeed at secondary school too, the main exceptions being the highly mathematicized science subjects. For convenience we may call these subjects of the first kind (whose schemas are like the butterfly schema) and of the second kind (whose schemas are like the invisible exports schema). *Mathematics is a subject of the second kind*.

We can understand the geography of Mexico without knowing anything about the geography of France. But understanding of the concept *place value*, often but mistakenly regarded as elementary, depends on all of the following concepts:

the natural numbers
order
counting
unit objects
sets of objects
sets as single entities
sets of sets
numerals, and the distinction between these and numbers
numeration
bases for numeration

And not only these, since all the above are themselves secondary concepts, some being of quite a high order of abstraction. To show all of them, with their interrelationships, would require quite a large diagram.

Another important difference between these two kinds of subject is in the location and availability of the examples from which the new concepts need to be abstracted. For subjects of the first kind, the examples exist in the outside world; and if they are available there, a person may be able to form the concepts unaided. But for the second kind of subject, the examples are themselves concepts, and these are not physical but mental objects. The process of abstraction involves becoming aware of something in common among a number of experiences, and if a learner does not have available in his own mind the concepts which provide these experiences, clearly he cannot form a new higher order concept from them.

In both cases, however, if the examples, whether physical or mental, are available, then as teachers we can greatly help a learner to form the new concept by grouping them together for him. In the case of primary concepts, if the objects are small we can bring them together physically; and if they are not easily moved, we can arrange a mental grouping by pointing. In the case of secondary concepts, we can similarly bring the ideas together in a learner's mind by bringing together their attached symbols. In the case of our imaginary man who has just received his sight and is at the beginning of conceptualizing his visual experiences, we can say 'Red, blue, green, yellow . . . these are all colours.'

Two ways of communicating concepts

Grouping examples

So far, we have been concentrating on the process of abstraction, which is fundamental to the process of concept formation. Arising directly from this is one of the ways in which we can help a person to form a new concept, by grouping suitable examples together for him.

Explanations and definitions

There is another way of communicating a concept which can also be very useful if the conditions are right. Suppose that we are asked 'What is cyan?' and we reply 'It's a colour: a pale blue-green.' This is a reasonable reply on the assumption that the person asking already has the concepts *colour, blue*, and *green*, and that he also interprets the juxtaposition blue-green as meaning a colour in between. In most cases these assumptions are valid. In the case of our imaginary subject who is entering this field of experience for the first time, we would first have to ensure that he had the contributory concepts *blue* and *green*, which could only be done by the method of grouping examples.

For a mathematical example, suppose that we are asked: 'What is a trapezium?' We reply: 'It is a mathematical shape: a four-sided figure in which there is one pair of parallel sides.' Again, this is likely to convey the concept provided that the questioner has the concepts *mathematical, shape, side, four, parallel*. If asked by a five-year-old child, we would not assume these, and would be likely to use the examples method.

This second method, which we may call explanation, does not involve new abstraction. It uses the concepts which the latter already has, and helps him to construct a new one by combining and relating these: so it can only convey new concepts of the same order as those which the hearer already has, or of lower order. A definition is a concise and exact explanation, which also allows us to distinguish clearly between examples and non-examples. For these reasons (which are good reasons), mathematicians like definitions. But definitions have the faults of their merits, which is that they are not always the best way to convey a new concept for the first time. Both definitions and explanations have the additional advantage that the newly constructed concept has, by its method of construction, ready-made connections with an appropriate schema.

For convenience we may call these two ways of communicating a concept, provided that we bear in mind that new concepts cannot be communicated directly. Every learner has to construct these anew in his own mind. But as teachers we can greatly help this process along: as indeed we must, if

63

children are to acquire in about ten years concepts which it has taken some of the best minds of mankind centuries to construct.

Which of these two ways is the right one to use will depend on where this new concept is in relation to the learner's existing schema. That is to say, whether the new concept is

of the same or lower order as } those in the learner's
currently available
of higher order than } schema.

Most everyday examples are of the first kind. The new concept depends either on primary concepts, which the other person has in common with us due to our shared physical environment; or it depends on low-order secondary concepts arising out of our shared social environment, everyday reading, what we see on television and hear on the radio. A child asks us what is an ostrich. We explain that it is a large bird with long legs and small wings, so it can run fast but not fly. He may think that this is a silly kind of bird, but he now has a very good idea of what an ostrich is. This explanation succeeds because we were right in assuming, probably without thinking, that he already has the concepts *bird, wings, legs, fly, run*. Because the method of explanation works so well in everyday life, we expect it to work also in our teaching. And so it does for most school subjects, certainly at primary school level, and for many secondary school subjects too.

But this is not the case for mathematics. Year after year, we require children to learn many new concepts which are of higher order than those which they have already acquired. So for our teaching of mathematics, we must carefully distinguish between learning situations of the first kind, for which the method of explanations is appropriate, and those of the second kind, for which it is not. And in the second case, we must systematically apply these two principles.

1 New higher-order concepts are to be communicated by carefully chosen examples.
2 We must make sure that the necessary lower-order concepts are available in the mind of the learner.

These may sound simple enough, but they have important consequences. From the first principle, it follows that:

(a) we must be clear what belongs to the concept and what doesn't.

Figure 3.6   Parallel lines

From Figure 3.6, which has been copied from a well-known textbook, children learn a restricted and incorrect concept of parallel lines, that they are equally spaced and of the same lengths. So they may fail to recognize lines as parallel where this is not the case.

Recently I met a ten-year-old child who said that in Figure 3.7 overleaf, the upper three were triangles, but not the lower three. All the examples of triangles which she had been shown were equilateral.

(b) We must ourselves be aware of the distinction between closely-related but different concepts. If we are not, we may confuse children at the outset.

For example, subtraction is often called 'taking away' in primary schools. The early examples of subtraction which children meet usually do involve taking away. Later, they meet questions like 'Jean is nine years old, Philip is seven. How much older is Jean than Philip?' When told that these are also take-aways, naturally they are confused, since the teacher is

Figure 3.7 Triangles

passing on his own confusion. Nothing here is being taken away, which in the present example would not be possible. This is a comparison. Taking away is one of the contributory concepts for subtraction, comparison is another. Subtraction is a higher-order concept, which a person has when he realizes that these two ideas have something in common.

Another common confusion is that between a number and a numeral. A numeral is the name of a number, so this is like confusing a person's name with the person himself.

A child who was shown this: 3
and asked
'Can you write a larger number?'
wrote this.   3

We may not make this particular mistake ourselves: but there are many who tell older children to 'Convert this number to a binary number.' What they mean is 'Write this number in binary notation.' Binary and decimal are different notations, not different kinds of number, and when writing a number in a different notation we do not change either the number itself or any of its properties.

Conceptual analysis as a prerequisite for teaching mathematics: concept maps

The second principle is even more far-reaching in its consequences. It means that we must, before teaching a new idea, 'take it to pieces', i.e. analyse it to see what are the contributory concepts. And to make sure that pupils have these contributory concepts, we must analyse these pieces, and continue thus right back either to their beginning in primary concepts, or to secondary concepts which we are sure that the children have. For it is at the beginning that much of the trouble lies. In some pupils, important foundation concepts are never formed, so that for them mathematics never is an intelligent or an intelligible activity.

This conceptual analysis the first major step in the application of psychology to teaching of maths. Teachers must first

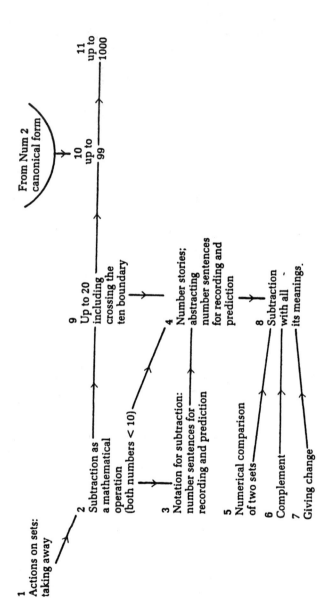

Figure 3.8 Concept map for subtraction

analyse the concepts so that pupils can re-synthesize them in their own minds. This is a huge job, and it is too much to expect busy teachers in classrooms (face-to-face teachers) to find time for this. But they are entitled to expect that it has been done by textbook writers, who may be regarded as indirect teachers; and it is important to be able to recognize whether or not this essential first step has been adequately done.

The result of a conceptual analysis of this kind can usefully be represented in a concept map. Figure 3.8 gives an example.

Concept maps (as the term is used here) differ from ordinary maps in two ways. They are directional, with arrows showing which concepts are prerequisite for which others. And where several arrows point to the same higher-order concept, the latter is incomplete until it embodies all of these earlier concepts. Concept maps are, however, like ordinary maps in that they allow us to make our own plans for arriving at new concepts. A writer may suggest an order, but there is no unique correct order. There are several good orders – and many which will not get the learner there at all! So concept maps are also useful diagnostically, since difficulties in learning a certain concept may well have their causes further back, in that other necessary concepts have not been acquired.

Another result of using a concept map for the first time in one's own teaching may not always be welcome, since (and I write from experience) one may find that one is teaching topics which one has never really understood. Fundamental changes may be needed in one's own thinking, and this can be hard work. But there are two rewards, which encourage one to go on. Not only do our pupils learn better, and this is rewarding professionally; but we gain new insights into the nature of mathematics itself.

Summary

1 Mathematics at school level does not require special aptitudes in learners. It is, however, much more abstract and hierarchic than most of the other subjects which children learn at the same age, and this makes special demands on teachers, including both face-to-face teachers

and those who prepare books and other teaching materials.

2 Abstraction is a process by which we become aware of regularities in our experience, which we can recognize on future occasions. It is in this way that we are able to make use of our past experience to guide us in the present. Concepts are mental embodiments of these regularities.

3 Primary concepts are those which are abstracted from sensory experience; secondary concepts are abstracted from other concepts, which may be primary concepts or other secondary concepts. The more times this process is repeated, the more abstract and remote from sensory experience the concepts become. 'Higher-order' and 'lower-order' refer to greater and lesser degrees of abstraction.

4 New concepts cannot be communicated directly. Each learner has to construct them for himself, in his own mind. But a teacher can greatly help learners to do this, if he knows how. Helping in this way may for convenience be called 'communicating a concept', provided that we remember the indirect nature of this process.

5 In this sense, there are two ways of communicating a new concept. If the new concept is of the same order as those in the learner's currently available schema, or of a lower order than these, the method of explanation is suitable. If, however, the new concept is of a higher order than those in the learner's currently available schema, the method of giving carefully chosen examples must be used. The latter situation is particularly frequent in learning mathematics.

6 Since in mathematics these examples are themselves concepts, it is essential to make sure that these are available in the learner's own mind. In order to plan for this, a conceptual analysis of the subject matter is essential. The results of such an analysis can conveniently be represented in a concept map.

Suggested activities for readers

1 For this you need a box of attribute blocks. (These are widely available in primary schools and centres of teacher education.) Starting with the concept map developed in Figures 3.1, 3.2, 3.3, expand this into a concept map to

illustrate the rest of the conceptual hierarchy which is embodied in the attribute blocks. Which concepts are secondary concepts, and which are primary? From your enlarged concept map choose further examples of the relationship *more abstract than*, and also *lower-order than, higher-order than*.

2 Make explicit the way in which the method of communicating concepts by giving examples has been used in the two sections of this chapter on abstraction and concept formation (pp. 52–60).

3 'Thick' and 'thin' really mean *thicker than* and *thinner than*. What examples would you use to communicate these more general concepts to a child? These are examples of order relationships. *Heavier than* is another example of an order relationship. Find some further examples, and draw a concept map to illustrate the formation of the concept *order relationship*.

4 If object A is thicker than object B, then object B is thinner than object A. The relationships *thicker than* and *thinner than* stand in a particular relationship to each other, which is called 'the inverse of'. Another example: *larger than* is the inverse of *smaller than*. Find some more examples of the relationship *inverse of*, and draw a concept map which continues down to primary concepts.

5 On page 59 only one of the hierarchies needed for constructing the concept *invisible export* is shown. Complete those for *banking, insurance, tourism*. The advantage of doing a conceptual analysis using this example is that most of us know enough to make quite a good job of it, although the concept is highly abstract. This may or may not be the case for mathematics.

6 Refer back to the sequence of numbers in Chapter 2, p. 32. What concepts are prerequisite for seeing the pattern, and thereby using intelligent learning rather than habit learning?

7 Draw a concept map for a mathematical concept of your own choice. This should continue down to primary concepts. If several persons try this exercise with the same concept, comparing results may lead to some interesting discussion.

4

The construction of mathematical knowledge

Schema construction: the three modes of building and testing

We have seen that an essential feature of the present model of intelligence is schematic learning. In Chapter 3, we also saw that if what we learn at a given time is to be usable on future occasions, abstraction and conceptualization are also necessary. So our meaning of a schema has now expanded to mean a structure of conceptualized knowledge. We have further noted that concepts and schemas cannot be communicated directly. Each individual has to construct them for himself, in his own mind. This is not too difficult with schemas in which all the concepts are of a low level of abstraction, such as the butterflies example. The more abstract the schema becomes, the greater the difficulty in constructing it, and thus greater the need for help.

Effective help of this kind becomes essential if we want children to acquire, in ten or fifteen years, knowledge which it has taken the best minds of mankind centuries to construct. Fortunately, the right kind of teaching can greatly help the construction of mathematical schemas. Unfortunately, as we have seen, the wrong kind can put people off for life. The fact that this help is necessarily indirect makes a teacher's task more sophisticated.

In the present theory, constructing schemas is represented as a goal-directed activity, that of a second-order system which we have called delta-two, acting on a first order system delta-one. (See Chapter 2, pp. 39–43). Given that we cannot help in the most obvious and direct way, by taking over the job of a learner's delta-two, how else can we help?

Good teaching is not trying to replace the schema-constructing activity of the learner's own delta-two, but providing as good learning situations as we can for this to do its own job. To do this, we need to know how delta-two sets about its task of constructing schemas in general, and mathematical schemas in particular. The latter can be more easily understood in the wider perspective provided by the inclusion of non-mathematical examples.

The term construction will hereafter be used to mean a combination of building and testing. These take place both at the delta-one level, of activity on the physical environment, and at the delta-two level, of building schemas whereby delta-one can act more effectively. When we are constructing a wall, building consists of putting mortar on the wall, and then positioning another brick or building block. Having done this, we test for spacing, alignment, and verticality. Building a wall is a goal-directed activity, in which construction alternates between building it a little further, and then testing that the change to the partly-built wall is in the right direction, i.e. towards the way we want it to be when completed. Constructing a transistor radio likewise involves building and testing. Building consists mostly of choosing and connecting the right components, while the crucial part of the testing has to be deferred until the end, since it consists of finding out whether we now have an apparatus which will receive broadcasts. To construct means putting together a structure, and in all cases, the structure is all-important. It is the difference between a pile of bricks and a wall, between a box of bits and a radio receiver; between knowledge, and a collection of unrelated facts and rules.

In the activities of delta-two when constructing schemas, we may distinguish three modes of building and three modes of testing.

The first mode of building knowledge structures is direct experience, from which a mental model is built yielding testable predictions. The second is social: sharing knowledge, and discussion, are major features of academic life. In the third mode, our existing knowledge gives rise to new knowledge, e.g. by the extension of known patterns to new situations. These modes are more powerful when used in combination.

SCHEMA CONSTRUCTION

BUILDING		TESTING
	Mode 1	
from our own encounters with the physical world: *experience*		against expectations of events in the physical world: *experiment*
	Mode 2	
from the schemas of others: *communication*		comparison with the schemas of others: *discussion*
	Mode 3	
from within, by formation of higher-order concepts: by extrapolation, imagination, intuition: *creativity*		comparison with one's own existing knowledge and beliefs: *internal consistency*

Figure 4.1

In conventional mathematics teaching, the main emphasis is on communication by the teacher of a method for doing a certain kind of task, after which the pupils practise using this method on further tasks of the same kind. Thus, only one at most of the six available means for intelligent learning is made available to the child, even assuming that the reasons behind these rules are also explained. It is no wonder that so many of them have problems. If we are to provide learning situations favourable for learners to construct their own schemas, these need to include methods and materials for bringing into use all six of these modes.

Mode 1: the importance of structured practical activities

The higher the building or other structure, the more important are its foundations, and this analogy applies with full force to the present discussion of knowledge structures. Schemas like the butterfly example may be compared to a bungalow, schemas like the invisible exports example to a skyscraper. In both cases, it is the primary concepts which correspond to the foundations. In the case of butterflies, these are available in the environment at the right time of year[1] and this is also the case for mathematics in its earliest beginnings. Children come to school having already acquired, without formal teaching, more mathematical knowledge than they are usually given credit for.[2] These are not sufficient to take the weight of the lofty abstract structures which we want them, with our help, to build. Nevertheless, they should be respected. It is not helping if we ignore or brush aside what children have achieved already, and by implication teach them that this is of no value or relevance to mathematics as it is done in school. The help they need at this stage is to be found in activities which help them to consolidate and organize their informal knowledge, and to extend it in such a way that it begins to dovetail with the highly organized knowledge which is part of our social inheritance. When this happens, they are starting to build the kind of foundations which will be capable of supporting a knowledge structure of the skyscraper kind.

As a result of the foregoing analysis, it has been found possible to devise activities involving mode 1 schema building which not only help children to build structured mathematical knowledge, but to use this to make testable predictions. One of the early findings of the Primary Mathematics Project was that children take much pleasure from finding their predictions confirmed by events. And if this does not happen, they like to be in a position immediately to correct their own thinking rather than wait for a teacher to tell them where they went wrong. This allows them to experience mathematics, on a miniature scale, as increasing their power to predict and control their environment. It also gives them greater control in directing their own learning processes than does the kind of situation in which they depend mainly on their teacher to tell them whether or not they have answered correctly, and what

75

they did wrong. With activities of this kind, the event either does or does not happen as they predicted, which tells them whether their thinking was or was not correct. And by returning again to the physical materials for schema building, they can correct their mathematical model, and their use of it. Examples of this kind of activity will be given in Chapter 6, which may with advantage be read in parallel with the rest of the present chapter.

Mode 2: the value of co-operative learning[3]

Mode 2 learning is co-operative learning, by exchange of ideas and discussion. This can be combined well with mode 1 learning, and extended into more abstract areas of thinking. If activities which embody mathematical concepts are done in pairs or small groups, children will naturally talk about what they are doing. In such situations they will be talking about mathematics, as embodied in these materials and activities. This has a number of benefits. First, they are putting their thoughts into words, in a mathematical situation. This is an important first step towards putting mathematics on paper, which is more difficult. Activities are also available which take the form of games, in which success depends largely on mathematical thinking. The rules for these games are largely mathematical, so whether a move is allowable or not depends on agreement about what is correct or incorrect mathematically. In this way, children correct each others' mistakes in a way which is much less threatening than being told one is wrong by a teacher. Trying to justify, or disagree with, a move on mathematical grounds means explaining oneself clearly, and this requires one to get these ideas clear in one's own mind. Simply speaking one's thoughts aloud takes one a step in that direction.

The activities based on physical embodiments of mathematical ideas provide shared sensory experiences which ensure that there is common ground for children's discussion. Other activities, in which symbols such as number cards are used, are more abstract. In this case the shared experience is partly at a symbolic level, but more importantly at a mental level in the form of shared mathematical ideas and experiences. The benefits already described continue to apply, with equal or greater force. Activities of these kinds are also described in Chapter 6.

Mode 3: creativity in the learning of mathematics

Learning in the ways described makes it possible for the natural creativity of the child to come into action. This is a resource which we expect to be used in subjects such as art, dance, drama. The suggestion that it is an important resource in the learning of mathematics may, however, come as a surprise.

In the context of mathematics, creativity means mental creativity: using existing knowledge to create new knowledge. We create also in the physical world. Almost daily we encounter new inventions, new kinds of car, newly styled garments – consumer durables and ephemera of all kinds. Outwardly this appears as an activity of delta-one. But delta-one has to be provided with plans of action before physical creation takes place. Invention and design take place first in the mind, and on the drawing board: then in the physical world. Here there is an interaction between mental and physical creativity – between the activities of delta-two and of delta-one.

Mathematics is mostly a delta-two activity. But the schemas, the knowledge structures, of mathematics provide strong support for many of the inventions which take place in the fields of science and technology. The jet engine, one of the most conspicuous technical inventions of our time, began as several pages of mathematical equations in Whittle's notebook.

Mathematics, like the arts, has an aesthetic quality of its own which gives much pleasure to those who can experience it. It is good if we can put children in the way of experiencing this pleasure. Since mathematics takes place in our minds, this makes mathematical creativity something personal; but communicating the results can result in a shared pleasure. Here is an example. (The activity the children were engaged in introduces the concept of multiplication, and is described in full detail in Chapter 6.)

Five children were playing, and each was provided with a small oval card and some small objects such as shells, buttons,

77

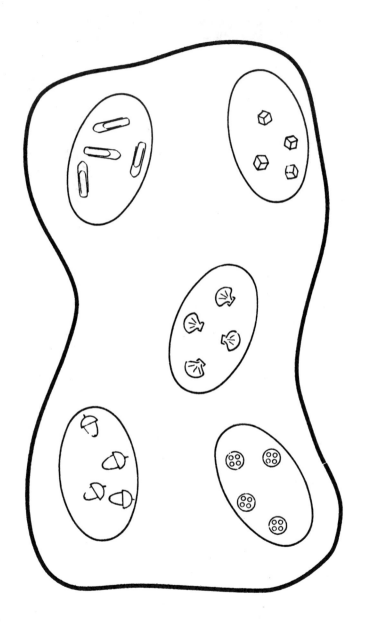

Figure 4.2

acorn cups. To begin with, one child was asked to make, on his oval set card, a set of whatever number he chose. The others were then asked to make matching sets – that is, sets of the same number – on their own set cards. The children checked each other's sets, and these were then brought together inside a large set loop.

In the present example, the first child had made a set of 4 shells. So there were in the large set loop 5 sets, each of 4 objects, as shown in Figure 4.2.

I said (pointing), 'Now we have five sets, with four in each. How many altogether?' Most of the children started to count, but after only a few seconds one little girl (this was a class of top infants, so her age was rising seven) surprised me by saying 'Twenty'. Since I didn't think she could have counted them all in so short a time, I asked 'How did you answer so quickly?' She replied (pointing), 'Two fours, eight, and two from this four makes ten. Then there's the same again – twenty.'

This incident gave me much pleasure, as it has to others to whom I have related it. It is an example of what mathematicians often call 'an elegant solution', and shows that we need not be high-powered mathematicians to experience and share this pleasure.

Creativity of this kind is based on structured knowledge, not on ignorance. So teaching of the kind which helps children to build up their knowledge structures does not interfere with their creativity: it provides resources. Amanda already knew a lot of addition relationships, so from these she was able to construct a multiplication relationship. The more we know, the greater the resources from which we can create new knowledge. Clearly it involves intelligent learning, not habit learning. But fluency is valuable, and must not be confused with habit learning. Amanda had her knowledge readily available, and was able to choose from the many addition facts she knew just those which were useful at that moment. By itself, it is often hard to distinguish fluency from habit learning. The criterion is adaptability of the uses to which the knowledge is put. A correct answer to 'What is 4 + 4 + 2?' could have been given by habit learning. But to select from all the possible combinations just that sum, and apply it to the present situation, evidenced intelligent learning combined with fluency.

Extrapolation of a known pattern is another example of

creativity. When a child can count 1, 2, 3, 4, . . ., he does not start from scratch when extending the pattern to 10, 20, 30, 40 . . . and 100, 200, 300, 400, ... Communication of these new patterns will start him off, after which he may be able to continue them without further outside help. If so, he is using his creativity to extrapolate his knowledge of the counting pattern. He may at the same time be extrapolating his concept of number, though initially it is good for further support to be provided in the form of physical embodiments of the base ten system of numeration. In this way schema building by modes 1, 2, and 3 can be combined.

Another example of using existing knowledge to create new knowledge may be found in the topic of multiplication. It is no small thing that once we know all the products from 1×1 to 9×9, we can find the product of any two numbers we choose. If the processes of multiplying numbers of any size first by a single-digit number, and then by numbers of several digits, are learnt as mechanical rules, little understanding and no creativity are involved. Children are simply being taught to function mechanically like a calculator, and for getting the answer quickly and accurately it is much better for them to use calculators. But the mathematical principles which make these extrapolations valid are of great importance and generality. For example, multiplying 37 by 4 is possible because four thirty-sevens is equal to four thirties plus four sevens. This is the case whatever the numbers, a property of the natural number system which forms one of the foundations of algebra:

$$a \times (p + q) = a \times p + a \times q$$
where a, p, q, stand for any numbers.

We do not expect children to make this extrapolation unaided. If they are helped to do so by good teaching, creativity is still being used, albeit in combination with other modes. And valuable meta-learning is taking place, about the nature of mathematics itself.

Schemas and long-term learning

Some of the reasons why schemas are important for intelligent learning have already been discussed, and may usefully be brought together at this stage.

- (i) They make possible understanding, and thereby adaptability.
- (ii) They provide a rich source of plans of action and techniques for a wide variety of applications.
- (iii) Shared schemas have important social functions. They facilitate co-operation on the basis of shared understanding, and plans which fit together to achieve shared or compatible goals. The shared knowledge of any given profession is an important example of this.

This list can be extended, with special reference to long-term learning.

- (iv) Learning is easier.
- (v) Retention is better.
- (vi) Future learning is also easier.

Learning is easier

We have already seen, in Chapter 2 (pp. 40–41), that when schematic learning is possible, it is much easier. This difference was investigated systematically in one of my early experiments over a four-week period, with two groups totalling over 60 schoolchildren. In this experiment, it was found that material learnt schematically was, when tested immediately after learning, remembered slightly more than twice as well as identical material learnt by rote.[4]

Retention is better

One day later, the schematically learnt material was remembered three times better, and four weeks later, seven times better. The difference in long-term recall was even more striking than in the short-term learning.

Future learning is also easier

The build-up of the schemas was spread over four one-hour periods, on four successive days. The new material presented each day was such that it could be understood in terms of the schema already acquired. When this had taken place, the expanded schema was available on the following day for the learning with understanding of that day's new material. This principle is quite general. When learning takes place with understanding, new concepts are formed and connected with an appropriate schema. The schema itself thereby expands, and after a period of consolidation we are capable of assimilating yet more ideas which previously would have been beyond the reach of our understanding. So our schemas grow by this combined process of assimilating new experiences to themselves, and thereby expanding.

The process is organic in quality. When a seed germinates, it first puts out roots downwards, and shoots with leaves upwards. These gather nourishment from the soil, and energy from the sun by photosynthesis. The combined result is transformed by the growing plant or tree into its own substance, including more roots, and more leaves. The increased root and leaf system are able to take in more nourishment than before, and so the results of past growth facilitate future growth.

Implications for teaching

These are twofold.

(i) To enable children to learn with understanding, we must wherever possible ensure that the new concepts embodied in the learning materials we provide are such as can be assimilated to their existing schemas.

(ii) We must give particularly careful thought to the foundation schemas in every topic.

The first implication can be seen as a straightforward expansion of the principles of concept formation, already described in Chapter 3; and the conceptual analysis, with the resulting concept map, provides a foundation for this approach. This will tell us what children should know already, if they are to be in a position to learn a particular topic with understanding. Complementary to this, we need to know whether they *do* know it. For this, we need some means of assessment which allows us to go beyond checking children's written work, in which it is often hard to distinguish between rote learning and learning with understanding. We need to be able to diagnose the state of development of children's schemas. How activity methods can help us to do this will be discussed in Chapter 6.

The second implication is particularly important for the following reasons. First, our schemas are highly selective. What can be assimilated to them is remembered so much more easily than what cannot that our schemas tend to be self perpetuating. Ideas which do not fit our existing schemas are likely to be ignored, rejected, or forgotten. This is one reason why it is important to start pupils off with the right schemas.

A second reason arises when we encounter new ideas which do not fit our existing schemas, but which we cannot ignore, reject, or forget. To understand these new ideas it is not enough to expand our present schemas. It requires us to make more radical changes – to replace some of our concepts by different ones, to make different connections. This process I call re-construction, and it is much more difficult. It is also usually unwelcome.

Our schemas are very useful to us. They are important parts of our mental equipment. So it is not really surprising that when we encounter situations that demand that we take them to pieces and build them differently, this is experienced as threatening, and we react with anxiety and hostility.

There are plenty of historical examples of this. When Pythagoras discovered that the length of the hypotenuse of a right-angled triangle could not always be expressed as a rational number, he swore the members of his school to secrecy. In his book *Men of Mathematics*, Bell writes: 'When negative numbers first appeared in experience, as in debits instead of credits, they, as numbers, were held in the same abhorrence as "unnatural monstrosities" as were later the "imaginary" numbers'.[5]

So we need to understand these defensive reactions in our pupils, for example when first they encounter fractions. These cannot be understood by assimilation to their existing schema, that of the counting numbers. As they understand the word, these are not numbers. They are not even told that they are being asked to expand their idea of number to include a new kind, still less are they systematically presented with all the concepts by which they can build up a schema which will be capable of assimilating the idea of a fractional number.[6] We should also be on the look-out for defensive reactions in ourselves if, for example, we meet ideas which suggest radical changes in our concept of good teaching.

So far as our pupils are concerned, we can help to save them from having to re-construct their schemas more often than is absolutely necessary by taking careful thought about the foundation schemas. Here is an example of how this may be done.

Multiplication is often taught to young children as repeated addition. For the natural numbers this causes no problem, and is probably the easiest for them to understand. But it causes problems later, for example when we ask them to learn how to multiply fractions. Here, the concept of repeated addition has no meaning. What is more, the children are seldom told that we have changed the meaning of the word 'multiplication'.

If, however, we teach children multiplication as the combination of two operations, this is only a little harder initially; and they now have a concept which can be expanded without re-structuring to include all the other kinds of multiplication they are likely to meet. This is how it was being introduced in the incident related on p. 79. (Please refer back to Figure 4.2 for what follows.) The first operation here is 'Make a set of 4 objects'. The result is a set, which is now treated as an object on which the next operation is done: 'Make a set of 5 such sets.' The combination of these two operations is equivalent to the single operation 'Make a set of 20 objects', and this single operation is called the *product* of the other two operations. This basic schema for multiplication is no harder to understand than repeated addition when it is presented in the physical embodiment described here and in Chapter 6; but the combination of two operations can be expanded without re-construction to apply to the multiplication of fractions, of matrices, and of functions in general.[7]

Schemas and the enjoyment of learning

During early experiments in schematic learning, a strong subjective impression was gained that children enjoyed learning in this way more than rote learning. To test this hypothesis, a group of primary school children were given material to learn which, though similar in the individual items of content, differed in the way this content was presented. One set of material was selected from the original schematic learning experiment and similarly organized; the other set consisted of further material from the same source, but random in presentation so that learning by the progressive build-up of schemas was virtually impossible. At the end of this session, the experimenter said that she would be coming back in a week, and children could choose which kind of learning task they would like to do. They were asked to put a tick at the bottom of their answer sheets to indicate which kind they wanted to do.

As expected, a large majority opted for another schematic learning task. There were, however, several children who ticked the other box, so on her next visit the experimenter asked them why they had made this choice. They replied that in the first set they had learnt, they had been able to see how all the separate things to be learnt fitted together. The second set looked like the first, so they thought there had to be a pattern, but they had not been able to find it. So they thought it would be interesting to see if they could find the pattern next time.[8]

Readers who are able to do with children some of the activities described in Chapter 6 will be able to judge for themselves whether these particular children find intelligent learning intrinsically enjoyable, independently of external rewards such as pleasing their teacher, stars against their names, and the like. Most children do, but this does vary between schools. In a few of the schools we[9] have worked in, we found that the children were watching our faces more than the materials we were working with, and were clearly trying to find the answers which would please us, rather than those which made sense to them in terms of the activity. There are some schools in which the climate is not favourable to intelligent learning: this problem will be discussed further in Chapter 8: 'Management for intelligent learning'. It is however good to report that the great majority of the children we have worked with clearly evidence a preference for intelligent learning. At the end of a session, we usually ask 'What do you think of this activity?' A frequent response from children we have been working with for the first time is 'We like this better than Maths'!

It has been suggested elsewhere[10] that in the evolution of *homo sapiens*, natural selection for intelligence has played an important part. If this is the case, then there are biological grounds for thinking that enjoyment of intelligent learning is innate, and intrinsic in the activity itself. Since human young are also dependent on their parents, and other adults, for a longer proportion of their lives than in any other species, pleasing important adults is clearly important too. One of the tasks of adolescence, however, is to reduce this importance, that of relations with peers taking on even more importance than before. Since we have already seen that learning with understanding reduces teacher-dependence and increases personal confidence, we now have developmental and social reasons to add to those already discussed in favour of co-operative schematic learning.

Summary

1 Knowledge structures (schemas) have to be constructed by every individual learner in his own mind. No one can do it directly for them. But good teaching can greatly help, and the more abstract and hierarchical are the knowledge structures (schemas) which are to be built, the more this help is needed.

2 The best help is not in trying to replace the schema-constructing activity of the learner's own delta-two, but by understanding how it sets about its task, to provide learning situations which are favourable to schema construction.

3 Constructing here means building and testing. We can distinguish three modes of building, and three corresponding modes of testing: see Figure 4.1, page 74. Briefly, these are:

	Building	*Testing*
Mode 1	experience	prediction
Mode 2	communication	discussion
Mode 3	creativity	internal consistency

These are more powerful when used in combination, so good learning situations are those which provide opportunities for using all of these, though not necessarily in the same activity.

4 Learning situations of this kind include:

   (i) structured practical activities
  (ii) co-operative learning in small groups of children
 (iii) those which use children's natural creativity.

5 When a number of parts are connected in the right way, the resulting whole may have important properties which would have been hard to predict from knowledge of the separate components. For this to happen, the right structure is essential.

6 Some of the properties of well-structured schemas are as follows.

   (i) They make possible understanding, and thereby adaptability.
  (ii) They provide a rich source of plans of action and techniques.
 (iii) Shared schemas facilitate co-operation.
 (iv) Learning is easier.
  (v) Retention is better.
 (vi) Future learning is also easier.
(vii) Intelligent learning is intrinsically pleasurable for most children, and does not depend on external rewards or punishments.

7 Because of the importance of children's schemas for long-term learning, we need to try to ensure that at every stage, the new concepts to be learnt can be assimilated to children's available schemas. This requires careful long-term planning.

8 Sometimes we encounter ideas which cannot be assimilated

to an available schema, and re-construction of the schema is required before this can take place. This is often unwelcome and difficult. For this reason, and to minimize the need for reconstruction on future occasions, particular care is needed with the foundation concepts on which a schema is to be built.

9 If the conditions described in 7 and 8 are not met, learning with understanding comes to an end, and only rote learning is possible. For mathematics this is so inefficient that further progress of any kind is unlikely, and pupils give up.

Suggested activities for readers

1 See Chapter 2, pp. 32–33. In order to use intelligent learning for the sequence shown there, what schema did you need to have available? A concept map would be a good way to present your answer. You may want to draw two, one for this particular case, and a more general one which applies to other examples of the same kind. You could also show the expanded schema, after assimilation of this new material.

2 Early numbers, below 10, need only simple expansion of concepts which children already have. But expansion to numbers beyond 10, and their representation in place-value notation, require additional concepts to be assimilated to the number and notation schemas before the representation of larger numbers in place-value notation can be understood.

One of these is the idea of a set. Next is the expansion of the idea of counting single objects to the idea that we can regard sets also as countable objects. Thus we collect a particular number of players into a team (which is a special kind of set), and we then collect a given number of these teams into a league (which is a set of such sets).

Think about the ways in which this principle is applied when we write larger numbers in hundreds, tens, and units using headed columns. What other concept(s) is/are required for understanding place-value notation: that is, the representation of units, tens, hundreds, etc., without

labelled columns? On the basis of your analysis, draw a
concept map for place-value notation.
3 Devise a physical embodiment of:

$$(30 + 7) \times 4 = 30 \times 4 + 7 \times 4$$

Where, in the usual way of writing this calculation, is this
'swept under the carpet'?

5

Understanding mathematical symbolism

The power of symbolism

The power of mathematics in enabling us to understand, predict, and sometimes to control events in the physical world lies in its conceptual structures – in everyday language, its organized networks of ideas. These ideas are purely mental objects: invisible, inaudible, and not easily accessible even to their possessors. Before we can communicate them, ideas must become attached to symbols. These have a dual status. Symbols are mental objects, about which and with which we can think. But they can also be physical objects – marks on paper, sounds – which can be seen or heard. These serve both as labels and as handles for communicating the concepts with which they are associated. Symbols act as an interface, in two ways: between our own thoughts and those of other people; and between those levels of our mind which are difficult of access, and those easily accessible. Though the power of mathematics lies in its knowledge structures, access to this power is dependent on its symbols. Hence the importance of understanding the symbolism of mathematics.

Symbols help us in a number of other ways too. Here are ten: there may be others.

1 Communication.
2 Recording knowledge.
3 The formation of new concepts.
4 Making multiple classification straightforward.
5 Making possible reflective activity.
6 Explanations.

7 Helping to show structure.
8 Making routine manipulations automatic.
9 Recovering information and understanding.
10 Creative mental activity.

These are discussed at greater length elsewhere.[1] Here I will expand on just two of them: those numbered 8 and 5.

Making routine manipulations automatic

Thinking is hard work, and the amount of information to which we can attend at one time is limited. Once we have understood a mathematical technique, if this is one which is often used it is a great advantage to be able to do it on future occasions with a minimum of conscious thought, and without having to repeat the conceptual processes which were originally involved. Symbols enable us to do this, in two ways. First we detach them from their concepts, and manipulate them in the same ways as before, but for the time being independently of their related concepts. This greatly reduces the amount of information to be handled. It is like moving people's names around on a seating plan, rather than asking the people themselves to move around a full-sized table. Second, we routinize these manipulations so that we can do them with a minimum of conscious thought. This is not only useful, but essential if progress is to be made, in the same way as writing and spelling words need to be routinized so that our conscious thinking can concentrate on the ideas we are trying to put on paper. This automatic performance of routine processes must, however, be clearly distinguished from the mechanical arithmetic, taught by drill-and-practice, which has in the past often taken the place of learning with understanding. A machine does not know what it is doing. A human being does, and at any time during the automatic performance of a routine process we can pause and re-establish the connections between symbols and concepts. It is essential that these connections are not lost. The power of mathematics is in its ideas, and the many benefits of symbols in helping us to access and manipulate these ideas will be lost unless we retain the ability to re-invest symbols with meaning. Re-attaching symbols to concepts restores access to the mathematical structures which justify the routines, indicates when they do not apply, and allows us to adapt our methods to new cases.

Reflective activity

By this I mean becoming conscious of our own thinking processes, and sometimes intervening in these, e.g. by devising new methods or improving the ones we have, or examining critically conclusions we have reached intuitively. Here is an example.

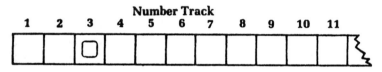

Number Track

Figure 5.1

When they are first learning activities which involve moving forward along a number track by counting on a given number of spaces, children often include the starting square in their count. Thus, a child with a marker on square 3 above who threw a 4 with a die might point to 3, 4, 5, 6 and finish on 6. There are two ways in which a teacher might deal with this. The first is simply to tell the child that when counting on the starting square should not be included. This may change their faulty method, but it does not bring understanding. The second, which we have found effective, is to ask them where they would finish if they threw a 1. I have not yet found a child who thought that this meant they would stay still: they always respond correctly to this case by counting on one space. Working on from this ('. . . and if you threw a 2?'), children correct their method by the exercise of their own reflective intelligence. They are starting from a case in which a correct answer is almost certain, and extrapolating it, each stage being consistent with what they have already built. This exemplifies what I mean by not trying to replace the learner's delta-two, but helping it to do its own job better. In this example, part of the help takes the form of talking about the method used:

relating it to verbal symbols. Another part lies in the powerful symbolism of the number tracks, which will later be developed into the even more powerful symbolism of the number line. And the right starting example was also very important in this particular case. This kind of teaching is much more sophisticated and professional than just telling them what to do. Long-term, it is greatly more effective.

Symbol systems

Though the powers conferred by the use of symbols are great, we are so used to them that we tend to take them for granted. The task of acquiring this understanding is also considerable, and we easily overlook the achievement of children in learning to speak their mother tongue with considerable mastery by the age of five. But we cannot overlook the difficulties which many children have in learning to understand mathematical symbols. For the children, this means to assimilate them to an appropriate schema. For us as teachers, this means not only to do this, but also at a higher level, to understand what symbolism is, what it does, and how it does it; and what, in this case, constitutes assimilation to an appropriate schema.

Symbols do not exist in isolation from each other. They have an organization of their own, by virtue of which they become more than a set of separate symbols. They form a symbol system. This consists of:

a set of symbols	corresponding to	*a set of concepts*

together with

a set of relations between the symbols	corresponding to	*a set of relations between the concepts*

What we are trying to communicate are the conceptual structures. *How* we communicate these (or try to) is by writing or speaking the symbols. The first are what is most important. These form the deep structures of mathematics. But only the second can be transmitted and received. These form the surface structures. Even within our minds the surface structures are more accessible, as the term implies. And to other people they are the only ones which are accessible at all. But the surface structures and the deep structures do not necessarily correspond, and this causes problems.

Deep structures and surface structures

Here are some examples to illustrate the differences between a surface structure and a deep structure.

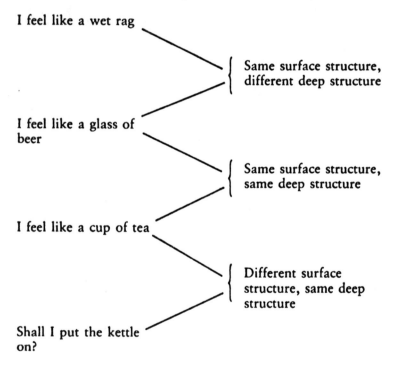

I feel like a wet rag

I feel like a glass of beer

{ Same surface structure, different deep structure

I feel like a cup of tea

{ Same surface structure, same deep structure

Shall I put the kettle on?

{ Different surface structure, same deep structure

What has this to do with mathematics? At a surface level wet rags and cups of tea would seem to have little connection with mathematics. But at a deeper level, this distinction between surface structures and deep structures, and the relations between them, is of great importance when we start to think about the problems of communicating mathematics.

For convenience let us shorten these terms to S for surface structure, D for deep structure. S is the level at which we write, talk, and even do some of our thinking. The trouble is that the structure of S may or may not correspond well with the structure of D. And to the extent that it does not, S is confusing D as well as supporting it.

Let us look at some mathematical examples. We remember that a symbol system consists of:

(i) a set of symbols, e.g. 1   2   3 . . .
                 1/2 2/3 3/4 . . .
                 a   b   c . . .

(ii) one or more relations on those symbols, e.g. order on paper (left/right, below/above); order in time, when spoken.

But since the essential nature of a symbol is that it represents something else – in this case a mathematical concept – we must add:

(iii) such that these relations between the symbols represent, in some way, relations between the concepts.

So we need to examine what ways these are, in mathematics. Here is a simple example. (Remember that 'numeral' refers to a symbol, 'number' refers to a mathematical concept.)

Symbols	*Concepts*
1 2 3 . . . (numerals)	the natural numbers

Relations between symbols	*Relations between concepts*
is to the left of (on paper)	is less than
before in time (spoken)	

This is a very good correspondence. It is of a kind which mathematicians call an isomorphism.

Place value provides another well-known example of a symbol system.

Understanding mathematical symbolism

Symbols	Concepts
1 2 3 . . . (digits in this order)	the natural numbers

Relations between symbols	*Relations between concepts*
is one place left of	is ten times

By itself this is also a very clear correspondence. But taken with the earlier example, we find that we now have the same relationship between symbols, *is immediately to the left of,* symbolizing two different relations between the corresponding concepts: *is one less than* and *is ten times greater than.* We might take care of this at the cost of changing the symbols, or introducing new ones; e.g., commas between numerals in the first example. But what about these?

$$23 \quad 24 \quad 25$$

Here we have one meaning for the order relationship between 23 and 24, 24 and 25, etc., and another for the order relationship between the 2 and 3 of 23, etc. And how about these?

$$23 \quad 2^3 \quad 2a$$

These three can all occur in the same mathematical utterance. This inconsistency of meaning is not just carelessness in choice of symbol systems; it is inescapable, because the available relations on paper or in speech are quite few: left/right, up/down, two dimensional arrays (e.g. matrices); big and small (e.g. R, r). What we can devise for the surface structure of our symbol system is inevitably much more limited than the enormous number and variety of relations between the mathematical concepts, which we are trying to represent by the symbol system.

Looking more closely at place value, we find in it further subtleties. Here we have numbers greater than 9 represented by numerals of several digits. (Reminder: a digit is a single-figure numeral, such as 0, 1, 2, . . . 9.) Consider the symbol: 572. At the S level we have three digits in a simple order relationship. But at the D level it represents

(i) three numbers $\quad$ 5 $\quad$ 7 $\quad$ 2
(ii) three powers of ten: $10^2 \quad 10^1 \quad 10^0$

These correspond to the three locations of the numerals, in order from right to left.

(iii) three operations of multiplication:
 $\quad$ the number 5 multiplied by the number 10^2 ($= 100$),
 $\quad$ the number 7 multiplied by the number 10^1 ($= 10$),
 $\quad$ the number 2 multiplied by the number 10^0 ($= 1$)
(iv) addition of these three results.

Of these four sets of ideas at D level, only the first is explicitly represented at S level by the numeral 572. The second is implied by the spatial relationships, not by any visible mark on the paper. And the third and fourth have no symbolic counterpart at all: they have to be deduced from the fact that the numeral has more than one digit.

Once one begins this kind of analysis, it becomes evident there is a large and little-explored field.[2] For our present purposes, it is enough if we can agree that the surface structure (of the symbol system) and the deep structure (of the mathematical concepts) can at best correspond reasonably well, in limited areas, and for the most part correspond rather badly.

Different ways of understanding the same symbol

The same symbol will be understood in different ways, according to which schema it is assimilated to. The word 'field' will be understood differently according to whether the schema to which it is assimilated is of agriculture, cricket, physics (e.g. electromagnetic field), general academic (mediaeval history, the plays of Shakespeare), or mathematical. If a person has all these schemas available (to varying degrees, unless he is unusually knowledgeable), what determines the schema selected?

A simple explanation which is sufficient to start with is to say that the sensory input, usually a spoken word or a visual symbol, is attracted to whichever schema is most active at the time. For a person with only two of these schemas, there would be only two contenders. And for a person with only one schema, there would be only one way in which he could understand what he heard, or saw written.

If a child has written this and we ask him to write a larger number, sometimes we get this response:

5

5

Such a child is understanding only at a surface level: at the level of marks on paper. At this level it is a perfectly good understanding. He knows the meaning of 'larger', and if we were asking for larger writing, his response would be correct. But he hasn't taken the first step towards symbolic understanding, since the essence of a symbol is that it stands for something else as well as for itself. Our request was not for a larger numeral, but for a numeral representing a larger number. An older child would be likely to assimilate our request to his schema of numbers rather than of numerals: that is, to a deep structure, from which he would have a correct understanding of our meaning.

Symbolic understanding

If we apply our general conception of understanding (see Chapter 2, pp. 42–43) to the present case, we have this formulation as a starting point.

Symbolic understanding is a mutual assimilation between a symbol system and an appropriate conceptual structure.

Now we are concerned not with the assimilation of concepts to schemas, of small entities to large ones, but with the mutual assimilation of two schemas, of two entities which are comparable in size and each of which has a structure of its own. When something like this happens, there is the possibility that one organization may tend to dominate the other. When the organizations are businesses, or nations, or political groups, the power struggles are often prolonged and destructive. They may also be sadly unnecessary, since a co-operative partnership could often have been for the benefit of both.

The power of mathematics is in the ideas. In the right partnership, symbols help us to make use of this power by helping us to make fuller use of these ideas. In the wrong relationship, a weak or barely existent conceptual structure is dominated by its symbol system, and mathematics becomes no more than the manipulation of symbols. Sadly, this is the way it is for too many children.

So how can we help children to build up an increasing variety of meanings for the same symbols? How can we prevent them from becoming progressively more insecure in their ability to cope with the increasing number, complexity, and abstractness of the mathematical relations they are expected to learn?

A resonance model

We need a model to support our thinking in this difficult and abstract area. The one I offer is based on the phenomenon of resonance. This is one which is widespread in the physical sciences, and many readers will already be familiar with it. For those who are not, the following experiment is a good introduction.[3] You need a piano (of the traditional kind, with strings!); and it is worth taking a little trouble to obtain access to one, since some of the effects are quite striking.

First lift the lid. Choose a note which you can sing comfortably, and slowly press down the key for that note so that the damper is lifted, but the string is not struck by the hammer. Now sing the note into the piano, stop, and listen. You will find that although you have not touched or struck the string, it is vibrating audibly. Repeat, with different notes. Now try this again with the loud pedal raised. In this case you will find that the string corresponding to the note sung responds most strongly, but others sound also. These are the strings whose frequencies are related to that of the note sung. (For a more detailed explanation, see the reference already cited.) Finally, raise all the dampers as before, and sing a vowel sound: say AAH. Repeat with others, lowering the dampers in between. Try other sounds, including short ones: e.g. a as in cat, i as in hit. In all cases the strings will resonate in combination to give back the sound of your voice with surprising accuracy. The reason for this is that a vowel sound is not a pure frequency, but a combination of related frequencies. So the piano strings which resonate are those with this same combination.

Other examples of resonance are widespread throughout science and technology. For example, radio and television receivers contain tuned electrical circuits which respond selectively, and are thereby able to choose from the many electromagnetic waves reaching our antennae those which carry the broadcast we choose to receive.

The starting point for our present model is to suppose that conceptualized memories are stored within structures which are selectively sensitive to different patterns in the same way as the tuned circuits described above. Sensory input which matches one of these wave patterns causes resonance in the corresponding tuned structure, or possibly several structures together, and thereby sets up the particular pattern of a certain concept or schema. We all have many of these tuned structures corresponding to our many available schemas, and sensory input is interpreted in terms of whichever one of these resonates with what is coming in. What is more, different structures may be thus activated by the same input in different people, and at different times in the same person. Different interpretations will then result, as described on pp. 97–8.

A related idea is put forward by Tall,[4] who has suggested that a schema can act as an attractor for incoming information. He took this idea from the mathematical theory of dynamic systems; but if we combine it with the resonance model, we can offer an explanation of how this attraction might take place. Sensory input will be structured, interpreted, and understood in terms of whichever resonant structure it activates. In some cases, more than one resonant structure may be activated simultaneously, and we can turn our attention at will to one or the other. In our television sets, the sound input is attracted by one set of tuned circuits, and this signal is amplified and fed to the loudspeaker; while the vision input is attracted by a different tuned structure, which is used to control the screen image. We normally combine these into one audio-visual experience, but can if we wish attend more to one

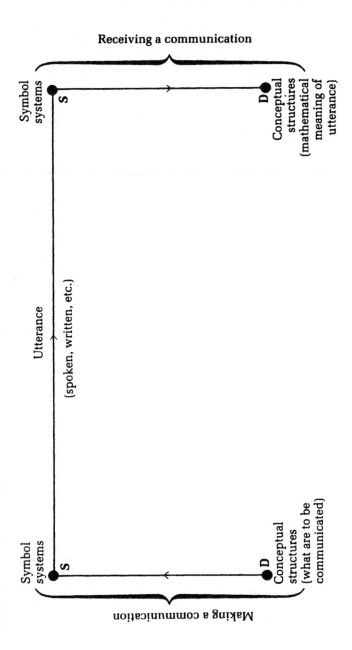

Figure 5.2 The path which must be taken by a communication if it is to be understood conceptually.

or the other. There are, however, cases in which one schema captures all the input. This capture effect is well known to radio engineers, who have put it to good use: for example, in radio and television circuits for automatic frequency control (AFC).

Figure 5.2 illustrates the process of communicating a mathematical idea. Note that in the diagram each point represents not a single concept but a schema, in the same way as a dot on an airline map can represent a whole city – London, Atlanta, Rome.

How can we help?

How can this theoretical model help our thinking, and what practical help does this suggest for our teaching?

Since communication is by the utterance of symbols, all communication, whether oral or written, first goes into a symbol system in S. To be understood mathematically, it must be attracted to an appropriate conceptual structure in D, in order that the input is interpreted in terms of the relationships within the conceptual structure, rather than those of the symbol system. (For example, 572 must be interpreted, not as three single-digit numbers, a five, a seven, and a two, but as a single number formed by the sum 5 hundreds plus 7 tens plus 2 units.) This requires: (i) that D is a stronger attractor than S. If it is not, S will capture the input, or most of it; (ii) that the connections between the symbol system and conceptual structure are strong enough for the input to go easily from the first to the second.

How, in our teaching, can we help these two requirements to be fulfilled in children's learning?

S has a built-in advantage: all communicated input has to go there first. And for D there is a point of no return. In the years' long learning process, if the deep conceptual structures are not formed early on, they have little chance to develop as attractors. And for too many children, D is effectively not there: it is either absent, or too weak to attract the input away from S. In these cases, all input will be assimilated to S: the effort to find some kind of structure is strong. So S will build up at the expense of D.

But this guarantees problems, for we have seen that the symbol system is inconsistent. Learning at this level may be easy short-term, but it becomes impossibly difficult long-term. This reveals a built-in advantage for D, since in contrast the conceptual structures of mathematics are particularly coherent and internally consistent. If these once do get well established, input to S will evoke more extensive and meaningful resonances in D than in S, and D will attract much of the input. Long-term, what is learnt in this way is much easier to acquire and retain. So an important part of the answer is that already given in Chapter 3: by a careful analysis of the mathematical concepts, we must sequence the learning materials in such a way that the new materials which children encounter can always be assimilated conceptually.

The model also underlines the importance of structural practical activities, using physical embodiments of mathematical concepts and operations. The structure of these physical events match the mathematical structures at the D level much more closely than they do the symbolic representations in S. For example, a rod of 5 cubes put next to a rod of 3 cubes embodies a visual comparison between the two numbers, in which *the number 5* can be seen to be 2 greater than *the number 3*. So we here have a situation in which the sensory input goes directly to the conceptual structure. By using first a do-and-say approach, followed by recording, the symbols then become linked with the conceptual structure after the latter has been established.

In the all-important early years, we should stay with spoken language much longer. The connections between thoughts and spoken words are initially much stronger than those between thoughts and written words, or thoughts and mathematical symbols. Spoken words are also much quicker and easier to produce. So especially in these early years we need to resist pressures to have 'something to show' in the form of pages of written work. And we can see an additional value in mathematical discussion, in its use of the spoken word.

It is also helpful to allow children to use transitional, informal notations as bridges to the formal, highly condensed notations of established mathematics. By allowing children to express thoughts in their own ways to begin with, we are using symbols already well attached to their conceptual structure.

These ways will probably be lengthy, ambiguous and different between individuals. By experiencing these disadvantages, and by discussion, children may be led gradually to the use of conventional notation in such a way that they experience its convenience and power.

A revised formulation

In the light of the foregoing discussion, I offer the following revised formulation of symbolic understanding as a goal for our teaching.

> Symbolic understanding is a mutual assimilation between a symbol system and a conceptual structure, *dominated by the conceptual structure*.

Symbols are excellent servants, but bad masters, because by themselves they do not understand what they are doing.

Summary

1 The power of mathematics is in the ideas; but access to these ideas, and the ability to communicate them, depends on mathematical symbolism.
2 It is also by the use of symbols that we achieve voluntary and rational control of our own thinking.[5]
3 A symbol system consists of:

a set of symbols together with	corresponding to	*a set of concepts*
a set of relations between the symbols	corresponding to	*a set of relations between the concepts*

4 Symbol systems are surface structures in our minds; conceptual structures are deep structures.
5 Doing mathematics involves both levels: the manipulation of deep mathematical concepts, using symbols as combined handles and labels. But for many children (and adults)

these concepts are not there. So they learn to manipulate empty symbols, handles with nothing attached, labels without contents.

6 Short-term, the surface structures may build up more easily since symbolic communications go there first. If the conceptual structures are weak or non-existent, the surface structures continue to build up at their expense, and a point of no return may be reached in which the input has no chance of being assimilated to a conceptual structure.

7 Learning at a surface level may be easier short-term, but it becomes impossibly difficult long-term because of its lack of internal consistency. In contrast, the conceptual structures of mathematics are particularly coherent and internally consistent, so long-term these are much easier to learn and retain.

8 The problem which so many have with mathematical symbols arises partly from the laconic, condensed, and often implicit nature of the symbols themselves; but largely also from the absence or weakness of the deep mathematical schemas which give the symbols their meaning. Like referred pain, the location of the trouble is not where it is experienced. The remedy likewise lies mainly elsewhere, namely in the building up of the conceptual structures.

9 So it is important for us as teachers to use methods which help children to build up their conceptual structures right at the beginning, and continuously thereafter. These ways include (a) sequencing new material schematically; (b) using structured practical activities; (c) beginning with a do-and-say approach, followed by written work only when the connections between thoughts and verbal symbols are well established.

Suggested activities for readers

1 Multiply 25 by 24. (a) If you know a short-cut, use it. (b) If not, first do it by your usual pencil-and-paper method, and then (c) use the hint in note 6 for this chapter to find the short-cut. (d) Consider the relative advantages of the short-cut and the regular method. (e) Think how you

would explain to someone else why the short-cut gives the correct answer.

The purpose of the foregoing is not so much to think about methods of multiplication as to illustrate two levels of mental activity. One is the delta-one level, in which we are centring consciousness on a task to be done. The other is the delta-two level, in which our consciousness is directed towards the methods themselves, devising new ones, comparing them in terms of their relative merits, and also testing their validity by mode 3: consistency with established mathematical knowledge. The first level includes routine processes, and also intuition, by which we arrive at new ideas or methods without knowing how we got there. The second level is that of reflective intelligence.

You are invited now to reflect on your own two levels of mental activity while doing (a) to (e) above.

2 Do, on paper, one or more arithmetical calculations of kinds with which you are familiar. Subtraction with 'borrowing' or decomposition is a good example to start with. Reflect on the relationship between the rules of procedure and the written symbolism on the one hand, and the mathematical concepts and relationships on the other. To what extent do you think that these are good relationships, in which the symbolism supports and gives good access to the meaning, and to what extent does it do otherwise?

Part B

6

Making a start

How to use teaching as a learning experience for ourselves, as well as for our children

The model of intelligent learning which was offered in Part I is applicable to all ages. It may usefully be applied to our own learning of any subject for which the appropriate mix includes a substantial component of intelligent learning relative to habit learning. (Reminder: the building up of a collection of useful routines is not the same as habit learning, but a valuable component of intelligent learning.) This description undoubtedly fits the two learning tasks facing most readers – not to mention many mathematics teachers who are not readers!

The first task is ourselves to acquire, if we do not have it already, a well structured understanding of the foundation schemas of mathematics – those which children need to build during their early years of schooling. Surprising though this may seem, those who have a clear and reflective understanding of elementary mathematics are in a fortunate minority. Most people know what to do, but not why. And elementary does not necessarily mean simple, as I found when I turned my attention from mathematics at secondary school level and beyond to mathematics as taught in primary schools. The importance of conceptual analysis, leading to concept maps on which to base a well-structured collection of learning activities, has already been emphasized. It was this, for primary mathematics, which first opened my eyes to the conceptual complexity of many of the topics in primary mathematics which most of us use – and teach – intuitively.

The second task is to understand the processes of intelligent learning both at a theoretical level, and also in their practical application to the teaching of mathematics in our own classrooms, both day-to-day and long-term. To aim for anything less is, in my view, to be less than professional in one's approach.

These goals will take more time to achieve than is available during most pre-service courses for teachers. But during this time it is possible to make a substantial beginning; and, more important, to find out how to continue learning 'on the job'. And one does not have to travel far along this road to find that the journey can be both interesting and rewarding.

As a preliminary to applying the present model to these tasks, it will be useful to review the three modes of schema building and testing described in Chapter 4. These are reproduced below.

SCHEMA CONSTRUCTION

BUILDING		TESTING
	Mode	
from our own encounters with the physical world:	1	against expectations of events in the physical world:
experience		*experiment*
from the schemas of others: *communication*	2	comparison with the schemas of others: *discussion*
from within, by formation of higher-order concepts: by extrapolation, imagination, intuition: *creativity*	3	comparison with one's own existing knowledge and beliefs: *internal consistency*

Figure 6.1

Experience has shown that a very good approach is a combination of modes 1 and 2, used in the ways described below. These may, of course, be adapted to the particular situation of the present reader. They are offered not as rules to be followed, but as a valuable combination of ways for building professional knowledge and skills.

At the end of this chapter are fourteen learning activities for children. They are offered here with an additional emphasis. Each of these activities embodies both a mathematical concept, and also one or more aspects of the theory. So by doing these with a group of children, both children and their teacher benefit. The children benefit by this approach to their learning of mathematics; and the teacher also has an opportunity to learn about the theory of intelligent learning by seeing it in action. Theoretical knowledge acquired in this way relates closely to classroom experience and to the needs of the classroom. It brings with it a bonus, since not only do the children benefit from this approach to mathematics, but it provides a good learning situation for teachers also. In this way we get 'two for the price of one', time-wise.

Observe and listen, reflect, discuss

In more detail, the method is as follows.

(i) As a preliminary to using them with children, you need to do the activities yourself, preferably with fellow-students or colleagues. At this stage it is useful to discuss their mathematical content. It is also good to go through the activity enough times to become fluent in the procedures, so that more of one's attention can be free for observation of the children.

(ii) Do these activities with some children. Try not to be actively teaching every moment: allow the children time to think for themselves. This will also give you time to observe and listen.

(iii) Reflect on your observations, and make notes.

(iv) Discuss your experiences and observations with a colleague, fellow-student, or tutor, according to circumstances. In these discussions it is useful to try to

111

> relate the observations, and your inferences from
> them, to the parent model. This provides a language
> for talking about the learning processes involved, and
> helps to relate the particular instances being discussed
> to an integrated and more general knowledge
> structure.

When some of these activities were first used in the way described here, the results were very encouraging. Experienced teachers on an in-service course said to the organizing tutor (not the present writer) that they had learnt more from these observations than from all the books they had read at college. In Canada, a teacher said 'It's as though the children's thinking was out there on the table'.

This was not only encouraging, but beyond what had been expected. Subsequent reflection and analysis in terms of the present model, and particularly in terms of the ideas discussed in Chapter 5, have suggested the following explanation.

What makes mathematics so powerful a tool for understanding, predicting, and sometimes controlling events in the physical world is the fact that it provides such an accurate and multi-purpose model of the physical world. *But* this correspondence is the one shown in Figure 6.2 by the lower arrow, not the upper one: between the deep structures of mathematics and the physical world, not the surface structures and the physical world. So when we give children materials to manipulate which embody these deep structures, we are doing two very important things. We are letting them experience, in simple examples, the power of mathematics to organize and understand the physical world in their own here-and-now. And when children are working with these manipulatives, they reveal the deep structures of their thinking more clearly than they do by words alone, still less by written symbols. Furthermore, the dominance of the deep structures in these activities helps to ensure that their spoken symbolism expresses these, rather than verbally memorized rules at a surface level. Children can sometimes be very articulate about mathematics in learning situations of this kind.

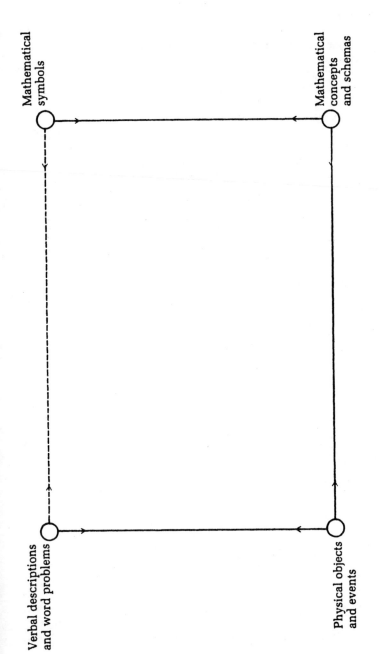

Figure 6.2

Some observations which have revealed children's thinking

Here are two examples. Readers who use the activities at the end of this chapter in the ways suggested will be able to provide other examples for themselves.

1 A colleague[1] was working on addition with three young children in a reception class. She asked them if they could say what five plus four made. All gave the same answer, nine: but each used a different method.

The first counted out 5 counters, then counted 4 more, and then counted all of them beginning from 1. From this we may deduce that he knew what the question meant, and knew how to use mode 1 schema building to find out something which he didn't yet have as a permanent part of his mental model. So he had a way of learning which did not depend on being told the answer, and which related his mathematics to the physical world.

The second used her fingers, and was seen to be counting on from 5, 4 more. This child still needed concrete support for her thinking, but was at a more advanced stage in addition. Counting on implies at least an intuitive awareness that the first set is included in the larger set formed by the union of the two sets: so it does not need to be counted again. Put like this, we can see that the step from counting all to counting on is more sophisticated than perhaps we give children credit for.

The third child just looked at the ceiling. My colleague said 'I could see how the other two got their answers, but I couldn't see how you did. Can you tell me?' He replied 'Five add five is ten. Four is one less than five, so the answer is one less: nine.' In my view, this is both good thinking and good explaining. This child was working at an abstract level, involving an inference between two relationships. He was also able to reflect on his own thinking, and was highly articulate about this. Though his chronological age was about the same as that of the other two, mathematically he was far ahead.

2 I was visiting a school in company with an advisory teacher. We were in different classrooms, but met for the lunch break. She said to me 'I'm thrilled with *Capture*. I've just seen two

children go from concrete to abstract thinking.'[2]

This game is described in detail at the end of this chapter. Briefly, it is a game for two children, using two number tracks side by side. Each rolls a die, and puts this number of cubes on her own number track. The one with the larger number captures the difference. After a while, these children had stopped using the number tracks. If (say) one threw 5 and the other 3, the first one just took 2 of the other's cubes.

Both these observations support the view that the use of physical materials does not necessarily make children permanently dependent on them. If they are ready to work at a more abstract level of thinking, it seems that they will do so. It is, however, good also to have activities for which abstract thinking is essential, to make quite sure. *Alias prime* and *How are these related?*, at the end of this chapter, are examples of these.

Fourteen activities for classroom use

The following activities are offered for use in the ways described earlier in this chapter. They are taken from *Structured Activities for Primary Mathematics*.[3] The activities themselves are as they appear there, but the accompanying discussions have been partly re-written for the present book. Since the English language has no pronoun which can mean either he or she, I have used these alternately in the descriptions of the activities.

In choosing just fourteen from a collection of more than three hundred activities, to include some suitable for all ages from 5 to 11, one of the features most strongly emphasized in Part A, namely their structure, has been lost. This was inevitable, but unfortunate. Where each fits into the overall structure can, however, be found by reference to the concept maps and accompanying lists of activities in the volume from which they are taken. For this reason, their reference codes are included for the benefit of those who have access thereto. They may otherwise be ignored.

Note that each activity is but one out of several for each topic. For any new concept, it is desirable to provide more than one embodiment. So the statements of the new concept(s) to be acquired, and of the abilities which should result from having this concept, apply to the whole of the topic, and not just the single activity shown here.

Apart from a spread of age and topic, the activities have been chosen with one other criterion in mind, which is that the materials should be easy to prepare.

In the full collection, photo-masters are provided for materials such as game boards. Only two of the present collection require these, which should not be hard to copy from the illustrations provided here. The other activities require only materials which should already be available in primary schools, and institutions concerned with pre-service or in-service education of teachers for children of this age, or which are easy to make using coloured card and felt-tip pens. If access to the photo-masters is possible, this will reduce the time required for making things such as number cards.

MISSING STAIRS (Org 1.5/1)

Concept An ordered sequence of sets with 'no gaps', i.e. in which each set is of number one more than the set before, and one less than the set after (except for the first and last sets).

Abilities (i) To construct a sequence of this kind.
        (ii) To extrapolate such a sequence.
       (iii) To tell whether a sequence is complete or not; and if it is not, to locate and fill the gaps.

Discussion of concept

If we cut half-a-dozen milk straws in assorted lengths, we can arrange these in order of length. But between any two we can insert another, which will conform to the same ordering. And if we take one away, there is nothing to show which is missing, or where it was taken from.

A sequence of counting numbers, however, has a special property. Provided we know where it starts and

---

finishes, we can tell whether or not it is complete: and
if not, which ones are missing and where they should
go in order.

This property can be shown very clearly in a
staircase of rods made from Unifix or Multilink cubes.

The activity

This is an activity which children can play in pairs after you have
introduced it to them. Its purpose is to introduce them to the
concepts described, in a way which allows testable predictions.

Materials   Cubes, in two colours

What they do
Stage a
1 Child A makes a staircase from rods made up of one to
  five cubes, all the same colour. (See Figure 6.3.)
2 B removes one rod, hiding the missing rod from sight.
3 A then makes from loose cubes of a different colour a rod
  which he predicts will fit the gap.
4 This prediction is tested in two ways: by insertion into the
  gap in the staircase, and by comparison with the rod
  which was removed.

Stage b
As above, except that in step 2, child B closes the gap, as
shown in Figure 6.4.

Stage c
As in stage (b), except that now child A closes his eyes during
step 2. So he now has to decide where there is a missing rod,
as well as make a matching replacement.

Stage d
The number of rods may gradually be increased to 10.
Children will often make this extrapolation spontaneously.

The first three stages may usually be taken in fairly rapid
succession.

Making a start

Stage (a)
Step 1

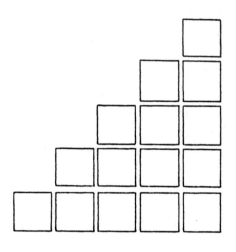

Step 2

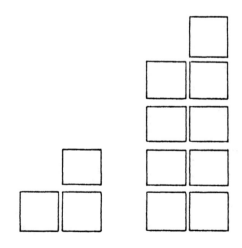

Figure 6.3 Missing stairs

118

Stage (b)
Step 2

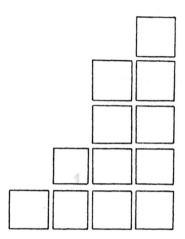

Figure 6.4 Missing stairs (cont.)

Discussion of activity

From this activity we can see that even such a simple
mathematical model as the first five counting numbers,
in order, can be used to make testable predictions. We
can also see the pleasure of five-year-old children when
their predictions are correct.

It is also worth analysing in detail the mathematical
model which children are using, particularly in stage (c).
There is more here than meets the eye.

STEPPING STONES (Num 3.2/3)

Concept Adding as something done mentally, with numbers.

Ability To predict the results of actions based on the mathematical operation of addition.

Discussion of concept

The word 'adding' is used with two different meanings, one everyday and the other mathematical. When we talk about 'adding an egg', 'adding to his stamp collection', we are talking about physical actions with physical objects. When we are talking about 'adding seven', 'adding eighty-two', we are talking about mental actions on numbers. To avoid confusing these two distinct concepts, we shall hereafter use other words such as 'putting more' for physical actions, and 'adding' for what we do mentally with numbers. We shall also avoid using 'action' for the latter, and use 'operation' instead.

The distinction we are making is therefore between physical actions and mathematical (i.e. mental) operations. Adding is thus a mathematical operation. Other mathematical operations are subtraction, multiplication, division, factorization . . . May I mention also that these others are not 'sums'? In mathematics, a sum is the result of an addition, although the word is loosely used in everyday speech to mean any kind of calculation.

The activity

This is a board game for two, three or four children. Its purpose is to give practice at adding, in a predictive situation, and with physical support for their thinking.

Materials Game board, as illustrated in Figure 6.5
Die, 1 to 6

Stepping stones.

Figure 6.5

Making a start

Shaker
Markers, one for each child (little markers, which do not hide the numbers, are best).

Rules of play

1 Players start from the near bank, which corresponds to zero.
2 Players in turn throw the die, add this number to that on the stone where they are, and move to the stone indicated. For example, a player is on stone 3, throws 5, so moves to stone 8. When starting from the bank, she moves to the stone with the number thrown.
3 If that stone is occupied, she should not move since there is not room for two on the same stone.
4 If a player touches her marker, she must move it. If this takes her to an occupied stone, she falls in the water and has to return to the bank.
5 The exact number must be thrown to reach the island.

Note. This can also be used as a subtraction game, to get back from the island.

Discussion of activity

Counting on is a useful method of addition while the addition facts (sometimes called 'number bonds', which they are not) are being built up in memory. This board provides visual support for this method. If children make the mistake of saying 'one' while pointing to the starting number instead of its successor, see the discussion on page 92.

When they are near the island and need to throw an exact number to reach it, initially children usually count on by pointing. But the time comes when some of them begin to say 'I need a three', showing that they have now acquired adding three as a mathematical (mental) operation.

CAPTURE (NuSp 1.4/4)

Concept The correspondence between subtraction and actions on the number track.

Abilities (i) To link mathematical ideas relating to subtraction with actions on a number track.
(ii) To use the number track as a mental support for subtracting.

Discussion of concept

Though subtraction might seem to be no more than the inverse of addition, it is in fact a more complex concept, derived from as many as four simpler concepts. These are taking away, comparison, complement, and giving change. The simplest of these is 'taking away', opposite of 'putting more'. If children have only learnt this one, they will have difficulty with word problems of the kind 'How many more grapes has Kate than Philip?'; so it is important for children to have practical activities which embody all four contributory concepts. The present activity uses the comparison aspect of subtraction.

The activity

This is a game for two. Its purpose is to introduce the comparison aspect of subtraction.

Materials Two number tracks 1–10
One die 1–6
10 cubes for each player, a different colour for each

Rules of play

1 The two number tracks are put beside each other.
2 Each player throws the die, and puts the number of cubes indicated on the track. The result might look like Figure 6.6:

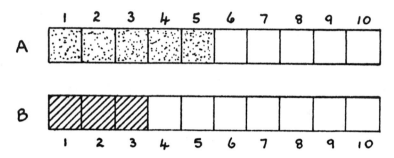

Figure 6.6

Since A has filled two more spaces than B, B must give A two cubes.
3 The cubes are taken off the track.
4 Both players throw again, and the process is repeated. Captured cubes may not be used to put on the track, but may be used if cubes have to be given to the other player.
5 The game finishes when either player has had all her own cubes captured, or cannot put down what is required by the throw of the die.
6 The other player is then the winner.

Discussion of activities

This is a straightforward physical embodiment of the concept described.

THE HANDKERCHIEF GAME (Num 4.6)

Concepts (i) Complement, i.e. the remaining part of a set when one part is excluded.
(ii) The number of this remaining part, relative to the number of the whole set.

Ability To state numerically the complement of any part relative to a given whole.

Discussion of concepts

An example will make these concepts clearer than the definitions (as is often the case). Suppose that there are six children sitting round a table, of whom four are girls and two are boys. Then in this set of children, the complement of the (sub-set of) boys is the (sub-set of) girls, and vice-versa. And relative to 6, the complement of 4 is 2 and vice-versa.

This concept forms a good bridge between the addition and subtraction networks.

It fits into the addition network if we call it missing addend: e.g.

$$5 + ? = 8$$

It fits into the subtraction network, if we ask, for example:

What is the difference between 5 and 8?

Counting on is a good method for both of these. Both relate to the comparison aspect of subtraction rather than the 'take away' aspect.

The activity

This is a game for children to play in pairs. (More can play together but there is more involvement with pairs.) Its purpose

Making a start

is to build the concept of complementary numbers in a physical situation which allows immediate testing.

Materials   Handkerchief
10 or more small objects such as shells, bottle caps, acorn cups, etc.
Number cards 1–10

Rules of play

1   The game is introduced by having one child put out ten small objects. (Suppose that shells are used.) The other children check the number.
2   All the children are asked to hide their eyes while a handkerchief is placed over some of the shells.
3   The players are told to open their eyes and are asked, 'How many shells are under the handkerchief?'
4   They check by removing the handkerchief.
5   The children then play in pairs, covering their eyes in turn.
6   Repeat, using other numbers of objects. For numbers other than 10, the children will need some kind of reminder of how many there are altogether. So, before putting down the handkerchief, a number card is put down for the total number.

Discussion of activity

This activity introduces the idea of complement in a physical embodiment. Children first see the whole set, and then part of it, from which they have to deduce the number of the part they cannot see. They are able immediately to test the correctness of their deduction. It is interesting to observe the various methods which children use for this. Using fingers is perfectly sound at this stage. Try to infer what is happening in their minds while they are doing this. Counting on, perhaps?

NUMBER TARGETS (Num 2.8/1)

Concept   That a particular digit can represent a number of units, tens, and later hundreds . . . according to where it is written.

Abilities   (i) To match numerals of more than one digit with physical representations of units, tens (and later hundreds . . .).
  (ii) To speak the corresponding number-words.

Discussion of concept

First, let us be clear about what is a digit. It is any of the single-figure numerals 0, 1, 2, 3, 4, 5, 6, 7, 8, 9. Just as we can have words of one letter (such as a), two letters (such as an), three letters (such as ant), and more, so also we can have written numerals of one digit (such as 7), two digits (such as 72), three digits (such as 702), and more.

The same numeral, say 3, can be used to represent 3 conkers, or shells, or cubes, or single objects of any kind. If we want to show which objects, we can do so in two ways. We can either write '3 conkers, 5 sea shells, and 8 cubes', or we can tabulate:

conkers	sea shells	cubes
3	5	8

Likewise the same numeral, say 3, can be used to represent 3 single objects, or three groups of ten, or 3 groups of ten groups of ten (which we call hundreds for short). We could write '3 hundreds, 5 tens, and 8 units'; or we could tabulate:

hundreds	tens	units
3	5	8

We are so used to thinking about (e.g.) 3 hundreds that we tend not to realize what a major step has been taken in doing this. We are first regarding a group of ten objects as a single entity, so that if we have several of these we can count 'One, two, three, four, five . . . groups of ten'. Then we are regarding a group of ten groups of ten as another entity, which can likewise be counted, 'One, two three . . .'. And as our mathematical learning progresses, we shall no longer be regarding these as groups of physical objects, but as abstract mental entities which we can arrange and re-arrange. We shall also have introduced a condensed and abstract notation (place-value).

These two steps need to be taken one at a time. While the first, described above, is being taken, we need to use a notation which states clearly and explicitly what is meant. Headed column notation does this well.

Also, because the correspondence between written numerals and number words only becomes regular from 20 onwards, we start children's thinking about written numerals here where the pattern is clear. The written numerals 11–19 are also regular, but their spoken words are not, so these are postponed until the next topic.

The activity

This is a game for as many children as can sit so that they can all see the tray right way up; minimum 3. Its purpose is to link the spoken number words with the corresponding written numerals.

Materials   *Tens and units card
              *Target cards
              *Pencil and headed paper for each child
              **Base 10 material, tens and units

*See Figure 6.7
**This game should if possible be played with a variety of base ten materials such as milk straws in units and bundles of ten, as well as the commercially-made base ten materials in cubes and rods.

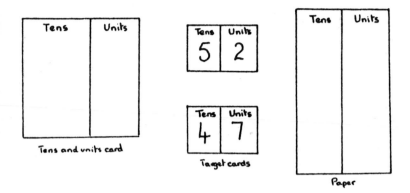

Figure 6.7

Rules of play

1   The target cards are shuffled and put face down.
2   In turn, each child takes the top card from the pile. He looks at this, but does not let the others see it.
3   Before play begins, 2 tens are put into the tray. (This is to start the game at 20.)
4   The objective of each player is to have in the tray his target number of tens and units.
5   Each player in turn may put in or take out a ten or a unit.
6   Having done this, he writes on his paper the corresponding numerals and speaks them aloud in two ways. For example, see Figure 6.8. He writes: 46. Speaks: 'Four tens, six units; forty-six.'
7   In the above example, if a player holding a 47 target card had the next turn, he would win by putting down one more unit. He would then show his target card to show that he had achieved his target.
8   Since players do not know each others' targets, they may unknowingly achieve someone else's target for

129

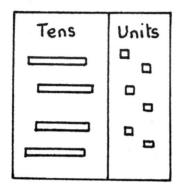 

Figure 6.8

them. In this case the lucky player may immediately reveal his target card, whether it is his turn next or not.
9 When a player has achieved a target, he then takes a new target card from the top of the pile, and play continues.
10 The winner is the player who finishes with the most target cards.

Notes

(i) If one side of the card is empty, a corresponding zero must be written and spoken; e.g. in Figure 6.9:

Figure 6.9

He writes 40, and speaks 'four tens, zero units; forty.'

And also, in Figure 6.10:

Figure 6.10

He writes 07, and speaks 'zero tens, seven units: seven.'
(ii) Players are only required to write the numbers they themselves make. It would be good practice for them to write every number, but we found it hard to get them to do it.

Variation

It makes the game more interesting if, at step 5, a player is allowed two moves. For example, he may put 2 tens, or put 2 units, or put 1 ten and take 1 unit, etc. This may also be used if no one is able to reach his target.

Discussion of activity

In preparation for place-value notation, it is important for children to have plenty of practice in associating the written symbols and their locations with visible embodiments of tens and units (later hundreds . . .) and in associating both of these with the spoken words. In this topic 'location' means 'headed column'; later, in place-value notation where there are no columns, it will mean 'relative position'.

This activity uses concept building by physical experience (mode 1). The social context provided by a game links these concepts with communication (mode 2) using both written and spoken symbols.

'MY SHARE IS . . .' (Num 6.2/2)

Concepts (i) Equal shares.
(ii) Remainders.

Abilities (i) Starting with a set of given number, to separate this into a required number of equal shares.
(ii) To state the number in each share, and the remainder.

Discussion of concepts

Sharing is one of the two main contributors to the mathematical operation of division. In the present context, sharing is always taken to mean sharing equally, unless specifically stated otherwise. Physically it is quite different from grouping. This may be clearly shown by taking two sets of 15 cubes or counters, and arranging one in groups of 3, the other in shares of 3.

If the starting sets are 16 or 17, there will be a remainder of 1 or 2 respectively – the same in each case. Here we have yet another example of how the same mathematical model can represent quite different physical situations. This is what makes them so useful, because multi-purpose; but it is also what can so easily cause confusion if we do not take care in the building up of these multi-purpose, higher-order, concepts.

The activity

This is a game for up to 6 children. Its purpose is to consolidate the concept of sharing by using it in a predictive game. This activity should be used after they have formed the concept, by sharing given sets of objects equally between varying numbers of players, without and with remainders.

Materials *Game board
**Start cards 10 – 25
**Action cards 2 – 5

'My share is ...'

START

Put out a set

of this number

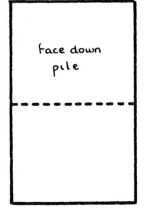

ACTION

It is to be
shared equally
between this
number of players

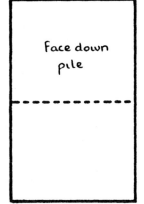

Figure 6.11

Making a start

> 25 (or more) small objects
> Pencil and paper for each child, and for scoring

*As in Figure 6.11.
**To fit the spaces on the board.

Rules of play

1 The start cards and the action cards are shuffled and put face-down in the upper parts of their spaces on the game board.
2 The top card of each pile is turned over.
3 A set of the specified number is put out.
4 Players then take turns, as follows.
5 The first player looks at the action card, and decides what her (equal) share will be (using pencil and paper if she likes). She then says 'My share is . . .', and takes this number of objects.
6 She may need some help, initially. Suppose that 19 objects are to be shared between 5. 'If you gave everyone 1 each, how many would that use? If you gave everyone 2 each, how many would that use?' (And so on.)
7 The correct number of other players take the same number of shares as the player in step 5. This will show whether she has decided correctly or not.
8 One point is scored for a correct prediction.
9 It is now another player's turn, and steps 2 to 7 are repeated.
10 When players are proficient, they may agree to play without pencil and paper, except for scoring.

Extension

The player in step 5 may also say what the remainder will be. If correct, she scores another point.

Discussion of activities

At this stage, we may leave it to children to devise their own methods. For larger numbers it is necessary to use known multiplication facts, and later they will be taught this method. However, with these smallish numbers there are other suitable methods, and I think that it is good to give children the chance to exercise their ingenuity. One of the features of intelligent learning is to use one's existing knowledge in new situations, and in these days of calculators this aspect can be given increasing importance relative to the skills of calculation.

Many children find sharing more difficult than grouping, so plenty of practice is necessary.

SLIPPERY SLOPE (Num 3.6/3)

Concept Extension of everything in the existing addition concept to cases when the sum is greater than 10, but not greater than 20.

Ability To be able to add across the 10 boundary.

Discussion of concepts

Adding past the tens boundary is an important step in the transition from quite small number operations, which can easily be handled in physical embodiments, towards operations with large numbers for which physical embodiments offer little or no help. As a beginning for this transition, the present activity uses physical materials and symbols together.

SLIPPERY SLOPE

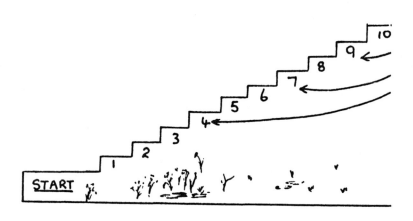

Figure 6.12

FINISH

Making a start

The activity

This is a popular board game for 2 or 3 children. Its purpose is to consolidate the skill of adding past 10 in a predictive situation.

Materials   Game board, as illustrated in Figure 6.12
Three small markers (three cubes) of a different colour for each player
Die 1 – 6 and shaker

Rules of play

1   The board represents steps up a hillside. Steps 11, 12, 13 are missing. Here there is a slippery slope, and if a climber treads here he slides back to a lower step as shown by the arrows.
2   The object is to reach the top. Each player manages three climbers, represented by markers. (When first learning, they may start with two climbers each.)
3   Players in turn throw the die, and move one of their climbers that number of steps up. They begin at START, which corresponds to zero.
4   A climber may not move upwards to a step which is already occupied. Overtaking is allowed.
5   Players may choose not to move. However, if a climber has been touched, it must be moved (but see also step 6).
6   If a climber is touched and the move would take him to an occupied step, he must return to the start.
7   If a climber slides back to an occupied step, any climber already on that step is knocked off and must return to the start.
8   The exact number must be thrown to finish.

Discussion of activity

This activity is the third of a sequence for teaching this important concept and skill. It provides visual support in the form of a number track. There is also a predictive element, since in order to decide which is the best piece to move it is necessary to compare the outcomes of more than one possible move. The game can be played at different levels of sophistication, and it is interesting to watch children progress through these. This also makes it a good family game.

Adding by use of a number track is easier than using cubes, which are afterwards grouped or exchanged for a ten and some units. However, the number track method does not easily extrapolate, whereas the base 10 material provides very well for extrapolation to hundreds and thousands. So the present activity needs to be used as one of several embodiments of the concept, including that just described.

TAKING (NuSp 1.7/5)

Concepts   (i)   Unit intervals on a line.
            (ii) The number line.

Ability   To use the number line in the same ways as the number track, in preparation for other uses of the number line.

Discussion of concepts

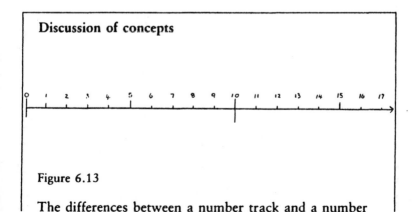

Figure 6.13

The differences between a number track and a number

line are appreciable, and not immediately obvious.

The number track is physical, though we may represent it by a diagram. The number line is conceptual – it is a mental object, though we often use diagrams to help us think about it.

The number track is finite, whereas the number line is infinite. However far we extend a physical track, it has to end somewhere. But in our thoughts, we can think of a number line as going on and on to infinity.

On the number track, numbers are initially represented by the number of spaces filled, with one unit object to a space. So it is rather like a set loop, in which the number of objects is automatically counted. Even if physical objects are not used, it is the number of spaces counted which corresponds to a given number. So the number zero is represented by an empty track, corresponding to the empty set. The number one is represented by a single space filled, which means that the first space on the number track is marked 1 and not 0.

On the number line, numbers are represented by points, not spaces; and operations such as addition and subtraction are represented by movements over intervals on the line, to the right for addition and to the left for subtraction. The concept of a unit interval thus replaces that of a unit object. Also, the number line starts at 0, not at 1. For the counting numbers, and all positive numbers, we use only the right-hand half of the number line, starting at zero and extending indefinitely to the right. For positive and negative numbers we still use 0 for the origin, but now the number line extends indefinitely to the right (positive numbers) and left (negative numbers).

Thus, the number line is a much more sophisticated concept than that of a number track. It gives strong support for our extrapolation of the number concept to fractional numbers, negative numbers, and onwards to more advanced topics such as irrational numbers and imaginary numbers. Two number lines at right angles provide co-ordinate axes for graphs. Truly, this beginning may be thought of as potentially leading into far distances of thought.

The activity

This is another capturing game for two, but a different one from that described earlier under the name of *Capture*. The former uses the number track; this uses the number line. Its purpose is to give practice in relating numbers to positions and movements on the number line.

Materials   One number line 0 – 20
3 markers for each player
Die 1 – 6

Rules of play

1   The markers begin at zero.
2   The die is thrown alternately, and according to the number thrown a player may jump one of her markers forward that interval on the line.
3   A piece which is jumped over is taken, and removed from the board for the rest of the game.
4   An occupied point may not be jumped onto.
5   A player does not have to move at all if she doesn't want to. (We introduced this rule when we found that starting throws of low numbers were likely to result in the piece being taken next throw, with no room for manoeuvre.)
6   The winner is the player who gets the largest number of pieces past 20. (It is not necessary to throw the exact number.)

Discussion of activity

This activity comes fifth in the topic which introduces the number line. The four preceding activities were concerned first with introducing the number line, and then linking it to concepts already familiar. The present activity is not unlike *Slippery Slope*, which is a number track activity. Like *Slippery Slope*, it involves mentally comparing a number of possible moves before deciding which one to make. Unlike *Slippery Slope*, none of the hazards stays in the same location. This makes the game more difficult.

Comparing several possible plans of action in the light of their expected outcomes, in a variety of possible circumstances, is one of the more important ways in which we use our intelligence in everyday life. So all games which involve this are helping to bridge the gap between 'school maths' and maths in the world outside school.

DOUBLES AND HALVES RUMMY (Num 1.9/3)

Concepts   (i) Doubling a number.
              (ii) Halving a number.

Abilities   (i) Given an even number, to double or to halve it.
              (ii) To recognize a number which is the double or half of another.

Discussion of concepts

We are now working at an abstract level, with numbers themselves as independent mental objects, as against numbers in some physical embodiment. We can do things to physical objects, and what we can do depends on their nature. Similarly we can do things to numbers, again depending on their nature. All numbers can be doubled; only even numbers can be halved, so long as we are talking about whole numbers.

We can also find relations between mental objects in the same way as we can between physical objects. A relationship between two numbers is a more abstract concept than the number-concepts themselves, so in this activity children are working at what is for them quite a high level of abstraction.

We rely on symbols for manipulating these mental objects. In the present activity, the number-symbols are written, the symbols for double and half are only spoken.

The activity

This is a card game for up to four players. Up to six may play if a third pack of cards is introduced. Its purpose is to practise the concepts of halves and doubles of a given number, independently of physical materials. It is assumed that children have already formed these concepts. If they have not, the concepts should be introduced using physical materials, and children given enough practice to become familiar with these.

Materials   *Two double-headed number packs 1 – 20, without the odd numbers over 10

*This just means that the numerals are written twice so that a numeral is seen right way up at the top, whichever way up the card is held.

Rules of play

1   The packs are put together and shuffled. 5 cards are dealt to each player.
2   The rest of the pack is put face-down on the table, with the top card turned over to start a face-upwards pile.
3   The object is to get rid of one's cards by putting down pairs of cards in which one is the half or double of the other.
4   Players begin by looking at their cards and putting down any pairs they can. They check each other's pairs.
5   The first player then picks up a card from either the face-

down or the face-up pile, whichever he prefers. If he now
has a pair, he puts it down. Finally he discards one of his
cards onto the face-up pile.

6   In turn the other players pick up, put down a pair if they
can, discard.

7   The winner is the first to put down all his cards. Play
then ceases.

8   Each player then scores the number of pairs he has made.
The winner will thus score 3, the others 2, 1, or 0.

9   Another round may then be played, and the scores added
to those of the previous round.

Discussion of activities

This activity uses mode 2 learning only: hence the
importance of establishing the concepts well beforehand,
using mode 1.

The first level of sophistication in playing this game
is, clearly, recognizing whether two cards form a pair.
What is the next level?

MAKE A SET: MAKE OTHERS WHICH MATCH
(Num 5.1/1)

Concepts   (i) The action of making a set.
(ii) The action of making a set of sets.
(iii) Starting and resulting numbers.

Abilities   (i) To make a given number of matching sets.
(ii) To state the number of a single set.
(iii) To state the number of matching sets.
(iv) To state the total number of elements.

Discussion of concepts

Multiplication is sometimes introduced as repeated
addition. This works well for the counting numbers, but

it does not apply to multiplication of the other kinds of number which children will subsequently encounter; so to teach it this way is making difficulties for the future. This is one of the reasons why so many children have problems with multiplying fractions, and with multiplying negative numbers. The concept of multiplication which is introduced in the present topic is that of combining two operations, and this continues to apply throughout secondary school and university mathematics. And as a bonus, the correct concept is no harder to learn when properly taught.

In the present case, we are going to multiply natural numbers. A natural number is the number of objects in a set, and we start with the concept as embodied in physical actions.

First action: make a set of number 5.
Second action: make a set of number 3.

To combine these, we do the first action (see Figure 6.14).

Figure 6.14

and then apply the second action to the result, i.e. we make a set of 3 (sets of 5). (See Figure 6.15.)

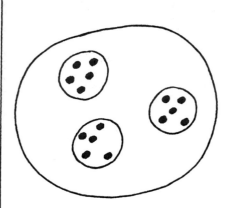

Figure 6.15

This is equivalent to making a set of number 15.

At this stage, there is not a lot of difference between this and adding together 5 threes, just as near their starting points two diverging paths are only a little way apart. But in the present case one of these paths leads towards future understanding of more advanced topics, while the other is a dead end.

The activity

This is an activity for up to six children. Its purpose is to introduce the concept of multiplication, as described above, in a physical embodiment.

Materials   Five small objects for each child, which should be different for each child, e.g. shells, acorns, bottle tops . . .
*Six small set ovals
Large set loop

*Oval cards, about 6 cm by 7.5 cm

What they do

1   The first child makes a set, using some or all of her objects. A small set oval is used for this. It is best to start with a set of fairly small number, say 3.

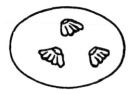

Figure 6.16

2   Everyone makes a set which matches this, i.e. has the same number. They too use set ovals and then check with each other for match.
3   All the sets are put in the set loop to make one combined set, which is counted.

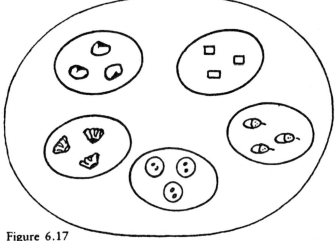

Figure 6.17

4   With your help, they say (in their own words) what they have done. E.g. 'Vicky made a set of 3 shells. We all made matching sets, so we made 5 sets of 3. When we put these together, there were 15 things altogether.' Or 'We made 5 sets of 3, making 15 altogether.' Or '5 sets, 3 in each, makes 15.'

5   The children take back their objects and steps 1 to 4 are repeated.

6   To give variety of numbers, sometimes only some of the children should make matching sets. For example, everyone on the same side of the table, or all the boys, or all the girls.

Discussion of activities

This activity embodies in physical actions on physical objects the concept of multiplication as described at the beginning of this topic. The first action is making a set of (say) shells, and the second action is making a set of matching sets.

Simple recording, including notation for addition, is introduced in the next two activities in this topic (not shown here), but in this introductory activity no writing is involved, to free as much attention as possible for concentrating on the formation of this new concept. Like place-value notation, it has proved on analysis to be more sophisticated than is usually recognized.

SETS UNDER OUR HANDS (Num 5.2/2)

Concept Multiplication as a mathematical operation.

Ability To do this mentally, independently of its physical embodiments.

Discussion of concept

Multiplication becomes a mathematical operation when

it can be done mentally with numbers, independently of actions on sets or other physical embodiments. At this stage we concentrate on forming the concept, using easy numbers.

The activity

This is an activity for up to six children. It is like the one just described, *Make a set: make others which match*, but now the process of finding the total number has to be done mentally. Its purpose is to start building the concept described above.

Materials *Five small objects for each child
          *Six small set ovals
          *Large set loop
          Number cards 2 to 5
          Pencil and paper for each child

*As for *Make a set: make others which match*.

What they do

1   The first child makes a set, using some or all of his objects. As before, a small set oval is used.
2   A number card is put out to remind them what is the number of this set.
3   All the children then make matching sets, using set ovals.
4   They cover the sets with their hands.
5   They try to predict how many objects there will be when they combine all these sets into a big set. This can be done by pointing to each hand in turn and mentally counting on. For example, if there are 4 in each set (pointing to first hand): '1, 2, 3, 4'; (pointing to second hand): '5, 6, 7, 8'; etc.
6   They speak or write their predictions individually.
7   The sets are combined and the predictions tested.
8   Steps 1 to 7 are repeated, with a different child beginning.

9 As in the activity before, the number of sets made should be varied, by involving only some of the children. All, however, should make and test their predictions.

Discussion of activities

In *Make a set: make others which match*, the physical activities were used for schema building. The activities came first, and the thoughts arose from the activities. In the present topic it is the other way about: thinking first, and then the actions to test the correctness of the thinking. First mode 1 building, then mode 1 testing. By this process we help children first to form concepts, and then to develop them into independent objects of thought.

In the present activity, the visual support which was available in the activity before is only partly withdrawn. They have to imagine how many objects there are under each hand, but they can still see how many hands there are. In this way we take them gently along the path towards purely mental operations.

THE RECTANGULAR NUMBERS GAME (Num 6.4/2)

Concept Rectangular numbers, as the number of unit dots in a rectangular array. (See Figure 6.18.)

Abilities To recognize and construct rectangular numbers.

Discussion of concept

Here is another property which a number can have, or not have. The term 'rectangular' describes a geometrical shape, so when applied to a number it is being used metaphorically. Provided we know this, it is a useful metaphor, since the correspondence between geometry and arithmetic (also algebra) are of great importance in

---

mathematics.

Rectangular numbers are closely connected with multiplication and with calculating areas. They provide a useful contribution to both of these concepts, and a connection between them.

The activity

This is a game for children to play in pairs. It uses the concept of a rectangular number in a predictive situation. Children also discover prime numbers, though usually they do not yet know this name for them.

Materials 25 counters with dots on them
Pencil and paper for scoring

Rules of play

First explain that the counters represent dots which we can move about. We could use dots on paper, but then we would have to keep rubbing them out. Begin by introducing the concept of a rectangular number by giving examples, such as that in Figure 6.18 below, and asking the children for other examples. The game is then played as follows.

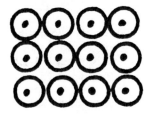

Figure 6.18

Making a start

1 Each player in turn gives the other a number of counters.
2 If the receiving player can make a rectangle with these, she scores a point. If not, the other scores a point.
3 If when the receiving player has made a rectangle (and scored a point), the giving player can make a different rectangle with the same counters, she too scores a point. (E.g. 12, 16, 18)
4 The same number may not be used twice. To keep track of this, the numbers 1 to 25 are written at the bottom of the score sheet and crossed out as used.
5 The winner is the player who scores most points.

Note If a child puts (say) three counters in a row and claims that these make a rectangle, remind her that they represent movable dots. Draw three dots in a row, and ask if these make a rectangle. I have not yet found a child who thought that they did.

Discussion of activity

Success at this game depends on predicting whether or not a given number is rectangular. Initially, each prediction is tested (mode 1) as part of the game. The time may come when they stop doing this. What do you infer?

ALIAS PRIME (Num 1.12/1)

Concepts (i) A prime number as one which is not a rectangular number.
        (ii) A prime number as one which is not the multiple of any other number except 1 and itself.
      (iii) A prime number as one which is not divisible by any other number except 1 and itself.

Abilities (i) To use these criteria to recognize prime numbers.
        (ii) To give examples of prime numbers.

Discussion of concepts

This is a negative property, that of not having a given
property. Children will already have formed this
concept while playing the rectangular numbers game. In
this topic we give the concept further meaning by
relating it to other mathematical ideas.

The activity

This is a game for up to six players. Its purpose is to introduce
children to the difference between composite and prime
numbers, and give them practice in distinguishing between
these two kinds of number.

Materials Three counters for each player

Rules of play

1   Begin by explaining the meanings of 'composite number'
    and 'prime'. These concepts have been well prepared in
    earlier activities, and children have usually invented their
    own names for them.
2   Explain that 'alias' means 'another name for'. In this
    game, all prime numbers use the alias 'Prime' instead of
    their usual name.
3   Start by having the players say in turn 'Eight', 'Nine',
    'Ten', . . . round the table.
4   The game now begins. They say the numbers round the
    table as before, but when it is a player's turn to say any
    prime number, he must not say its usual name, but say
    'Prime' instead.
5   The next player must remember the number which wasn't
    spoken, and say the next one. Thus the game would
    begin (assuming no mistake) 'Eight', 'Nine', 'Ten', 'Prime',
    'Twelve', 'Prime', 'Fourteen', 'Fifteen', 'Sixteen', 'Prime',
    Eighteen' and so on.
6   Any player who makes a mistake loses a life – i.e. one of

153

his counters. Failing to say 'Prime', or saying the wrong composite number, are both mistakes.

7 When a player has lost all his lives he is out of the game, and acts as an umpire.

8 The winner is the last player to be left in the game.

Note. When the players are experienced, they may begin counting at 'One'. This gives rather a lot of primes for beginners.

Discussion of activity

The concept of a prime number was implicit in the rectangular numbers game, when children encountered numbers which are not rectangular numbers. Here this negative property is made explicit and given a name. *Alias Prime* centres attention on prime numbers in a game based on this concept, and the concept is tested by mode 2 (comparison with the schemas of others, leading sometimes to discussion).

Primes were initially conceptualized in relation to rectangular numbers, which is a physical and spatial metaphor. In this activity they are thought of in a different way, that of not being multiples. They are therefore not divisible except by 1 and themselves. Multiplication and division are abstract mathematical operations, so the concept of a prime has now become independent of its physical/spatial beginnings.

This game strongly involves the activity of reflective intelligence, and requires much concentration. As the numbers get larger, beyond those in the usually-known multiplication tables, players have to find other ways of deciding whether a number is prime or composite. How about 51, for example: prime or composite? How do we know?

HOW ARE THESE RELATED? (Num 1.14/2)

Concept That all numbers are related, in many ways.

Ability   To find several relationships between two given
numbers.

Discussion of concept

One of the major emphases of the present approach is
that learning mathematics involves learning, not isolated
facts, but a connected knowledge structure. Here we
make explicit a very general property of numbers: that
every number is related to every other number, not just
in one way but many. Indeed, the only limits to how
many relationships we can find are those of time and
patience.

The activity

This is a game for a small group.

Materials   A bowl of counters, say 3 per player
A pack of number cards (or any other way of
generating assorted numbers). How high they
should go depends on the ability of the players.

Rules of play

1   The first two cards are turned over, e.g. 25 and 7.
2   Each player in turn has to say how they are related.
e.g. '25 is more than 7.'
      '25 is 18 more than 7.'
      '3 sevens plus 4 makes 25.'
      'Both 25 and 7 are odd numbers.'
      'The sum of 25 and 7 is an even number.' Etc.
3   Each time a player makes a new and correct statement,
the others say 'Agree' and he takes a counter.
4   If it has been used already, the others say, 'Tell us
something new'.
5   If an incorrect statement is made, they say, 'Tell us
something true'.
6   When all the counters have been taken, many different

properties and relationships have been stated about the same number.

7 The player with the most counters is the winner.

8 The game may then be played with a different number.

Discussion of activity

This activity develops fluency and inventiveness in the handling of numbers. It also increases the interconnections within children's schemas. There is much use of mode 3 activity – the creative use of existing knowledge to find new relationships. Testing is by mode 2, agreement and if necessary discussion, which in turn is based on mode 3 – testing by consistency with what is already known.

Summary

1 Our own teaching can be used as a learning experience for ourselves, as well as for our children. This has several advantages:
  (i)   Theory learnt in this way is closely related to the day-to-day needs of the classroom.
  (ii) We get 'two for the price of one', time-wise.
  (iii) Our own learning can continue in this way for many years, and thus compensate for shortage of time during pre-service preparation for teaching.

2 Activities of the kind exemplified in this chapter help to make this possible, since the physical materials externalize childrens thinking at this stage much better than their written work. Also, their discussions based on these materials are often highly articulate.

3 Application of the model described in Part I to one's own learning may be summarized in the reminders:

OBSERVE AND LISTEN   REFLECT   DISCUSS

7

The contents and structure of primary mathematics

Knowledge, plans, and skills

By knowledge I mean structured knowledge, not collections of isolated facts such as form the content of many television quiz shows. We already know that the latter are of low adaptability, as is well illustrated by the following example from Rees.[1] Craft apprentices had learnt at school that the area of a circle is given by the formula πr^2, where r is its radius. They needed to calculate the area of cross-section of a given piece of wire, so they began by measuring its thickness. This gives the diameter of the circular cross-section, not the radius. No problem, you may think: they know that the radius of a circle is half the length of a diameter, so if they know the diameter they can easily find the radius and apply the formula. But hard though it is to believe, many of these apprentices could not do this. Though they had the necessary facts, they were not able to combine them to make a plan for dealing with the requirements of this new situation.

The practical importance of structured knowledge, as a foundation for relational understanding, was well put by a mature student at the Polytechnic of the South Bank, after a talk given there about relational and instrumental understanding. He said, 'Instrumental understanding, which is what I was given at school, only enabled me to deal with yesterday's technology. This is why I've had to come back to college and take evening classes, to get the relational understanding which will enable me to cope with the technology of the future.'

This student had become aware of the inadequacy of learning which does not go beyond the memorizing of facts and rules,

157

together with practice in using these. Moreover, he knew that there was an alternative, and that this was what he needed. More important still, he had the confidence in his own ability to acquire the kind of knowledge which led him to undertake the evening course where I met him. Unfortunately, this is not always the case. Many have had their confidence destroyed because they think that they 'can't do maths', as was evidenced by the survey quoted in Chapter 1. It would encourage them to know that what they failed at probably was not mathematics, but a look-alike under the same name which, as is often the case, was of much less worth.

Though structured knowledge is the first requirement, it is only the beginning. Next we need plans of action. These are what we have to do to reach a particular goal from a particular starting point. In present context, both the goal and the starting point are mathematical, and the plans are plans for mental action (though they may usefully be represented on paper). It will be instructive to identify the plans involved in doing some of the activities provided in Chapter 6. In all of them, as in everyday life, an important feature of a successful plan is to stay within the constraints of the situation. When driving, for example, these are both physical (we have to stay on the road: the car will not cross ploughed fields or climb walls) and social (we stop at red traffic lights, and drive on whichever side of the road is socially agreed in the country where we are). In mathematics, the constraints are those of an agreed body of knowledge, together with agreed ways of representing this. So every time we make a move, it is tested for consistency with this body of knowledge (mode 3 testing). (In the mathematics look-alike mentioned above, the constraints are arbitrary rules without reasons.) To us as adults, constraints of this kind are so familiar that we take them for granted: hence the need, as teachers, to make them conscious by reflecting on them.

The particular details of the plans will, of course, vary between activities, and between players at different levels of sophistication. *Slippery Slope* is a good situation in which to observe the latter. For example, beginners often do not see the advantage of putting several 'climbers' on the board early in the game, so that they have a choice of moves for a given throw of the die. However, when they do so, and have three climbers to manage, a superordinate plan is now required: a plan for each climber (i.e. a move to the step indicated by the fall of the die and the mathematical constraints embodied in the game), and a comparison of these plans in order to choose the most advantageous. This is one of the ways in which we use our intelligence in everyday life. It is also good exercise for reflective intelligence.

Knowledge, and plans based on knowledge, are necessary but still not sufficient. The third requirement is skill: that is, being able to put our plans easily and accurately into action, with a minimum of conscious attention except when non-routine situations are encountered. Knowledge then allows us to adapt existing plans, or devise new ones. The latter takes time, and is not always easy. So the best combination with which to equip children is a firm foundation of well-structured knowledge, together with a good repertoire of routine plans for frequently-encountered tasks, these plans being frequently practised in a variety of situations until they become skills.

Activities for developing skills

Nearly all games are good for this, since they provide constantly changing situations in which players have both to come up with the relevant bit of mathematical knowledge, and put this into action appropriate for the context of the game. It will be worth reviewing, for instance, *The rectangular numbers game*, and *Alias prime*, with this aspect in mind.

There are, however, some skills which are so widely used, and also form the basis for other skills, that it is worth giving time to developing a high degree of fluency in these once children have a good grasp of the concepts. Multiplying any required pair of single-digit numbers is one of these.

A question which is often put, when one is emphasizing the importance of learning with understanding, is 'Are you saying they shouldn't learn their multiplication tables, then?' My own answer is that I wouldn't think it sensible to make children learn to spell words they didn't understand the meaning of, and neither would I teach multiplication tables in this way. The result is children who can add and multiply well at a mechanical level, but when given a simple problem still have to ask 'Please, miss, is it an add or a multiply?' However, children do need to be able to spell fluently if they are to be able to use writing for putting ideas on paper, and give thought to choosing the best words to express their meaning. Likewise with multiplication. Once children understand multiplication, and having learnt addition and multiplication in practical situations can distinguish which is the appropriate mathematics for a given situation, then they do need to know their multiplication tables, and time is well spent in practising these until fluent recall is attained. Here is one of a group of activities which were devised for this purpose.

CARDS ON THE TABLE (Num 5.6/4)

Concepts (i) Product tables, as an organized collection of ready-for-use results.
(ii) The complete set of products, up to 10 × 10.

Abilities (i) To recall easily and accurately whatever results are needed for a particular job.
(ii) To build new results from those which are already known.

The activity

This is an activity for children in pairs; as many pairs as you have materials for. They may with advantage make their own, and practise in odd times which might otherwise be wasted. Its purpose is to practise fluent recall of all their product results up to 10 × 10.

Materials 9 sets of symbol cards, each with 10 cards in each set, from 2 × 1 to 10 × 10
One multiplication table and L card for each pair (see Figure 7.1)

What they do

1 In each pair, one child has in his hand a single pack of cards, shuffled and face-down. The other has on the table his multiplication table and L-card.

1	2	3	4	5	6	7	8	9	10
2	4	6	8	10	12	14	16	18	20
3	6	9	12	15	18	21	24	27	30
4	8	12	16	20	24	28	32	36	40
5	10	15	20	25	30	35	40	45	50
6	12	18	24	30	36	42	48	54	60
7	14	21	28	35	42	49	56	63	70
8	16	24	32	40	48	56	64	72	80
9	18	27	36	45	54	63	72	81	90
10	20	30	40	50	60	70	80	90	100

Figure 7.1

2   Child A looks at the top card, say 4 × 7, and tries to recall this result. Child B then checks by using his multiplication square and L-card. This is done by placing the L-card on the multiplication square as shown in Figure 7.2.

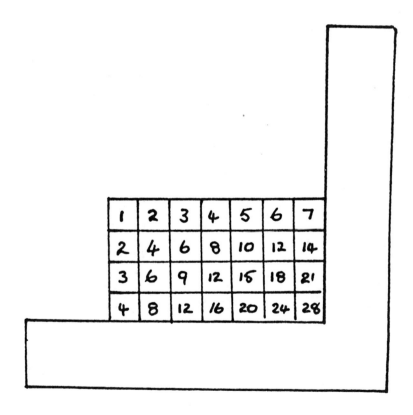

Figure 7.2

3   If A's answer was correct, this card is put on the table. If incorrect, it is put at the bottom of the pile in his hand so

that it will appear again later.

4 A continues until all the cards are on the table. This method gives extra practice with the cards he got wrong.

5 Steps 1 to 4 are repeated until A makes no mistake, and all his cards are put down first time.

6 The children then change roles, and repeat steps 1 to 5.

7 Steps 1 to 5 are then, possibly at some other time, repeated with a different pack until all the packs are known.

8 The foregoing may be repeated using two packs mixed together.

9 The final stage is to mix all the packs. Each child then takes from these a pack of 10 mixed cards, and repeats steps 1 to 5 with this pack.

10 This activity should be continued over quite a long period: say, one new pack a week, with revision of earlier packs, including mixed packs.

Discussion of activity

It is tempting to write the results on the back of the cards; e.g. to write 18 on the back of 6×3. I suggest that it is better not to do this, since it is a step in the direction of rote memory.

In its present form, each time they use the multiplication square and L-card they are relating what they are learning to a structure. The number in the bottom right-hand corner of the rectangle shown by the L-card is the number of squares in the rectangle, and the squares in this rectangle correspond to the pattern of dots in the rectangular number game.

The place of written work

Teachers who understand the importance of a strong foundation of practical and oral work will appreciate the paragraph in the Cockcroft report in which we read

... albeit with the best of intentions, some parents can
exert undesirable pressure on teachers to introduce written
recording of mathematics, and especially 'sums', at too
early a stage, because they believe that the written record is
a necessary stage of a child's progress.
... A premature start on formal written arithmetic is likely
to delay progress rather than hasten it.[2]

The foregoing observation is closely in accord with the
present theoretical model. However, the word 'premature' is
important, with its implication that written work does have a
place when the appropriate degree of maturity has been reached
in children's thinking. So what is this place, and what degree of
maturity is needed for written work to be a help rather than a
hindrance? Writing is putting thoughts on paper, so:

(i) Clearly children need the thoughts, i.e. the conceptual
    structures built and tested by practical experience and
    oral work in the ways already described and
    exemplified.
(ii) They need to be able to form the written symbols
    fluently enough for these actions not to require too
    much effort. Most of our conscious attention needs to
    be available for the thinking process. This is one of
    the reasons why plenty of oral work is useful: once
    children can speak, saying the mathematical words is
    normally effortless (though long words like
    'perpendicular' may need a little practice initially).
    Learning to write numerals and other mathematical
    symbols fluently needs first to be practised as a
    separate skill from the mathematics itself.
(iii) We need strongly established mathematical schemas,
    so that the conceptual structure always dominates the
    symbolic structure. (See chapter 5.)

Written work may usefully be introduced, initially in quite
a small way, at any stage of children's learning when the
foregoing requirements are satisfied, and when it serves one or
more useful purposes. These include:

1 *Reducing cognitive strain.* By 'unloading' some of the

ideas we are using onto paper, we have less to carry in our mind at a time. A simple example of this is in *The Handkerchief Game* (p. 125), when the total number of objects is shown by a numeral on a card, so that the children can concentrate on working out in their minds how many of this total are hidden by the handkerchief. This 'unloading' function becomes indispensable when we are doing a long calculation, or a long chain of reasoning. It also enables us easily to refer back to earlier steps in our thinking.

2 *Showing structure*. Compare these two ways of writing the same number.

Roman numeral	*Hindu-Arabic numeral*
MMCDLXXVIII	2478

The advantages of place-value notation become even more apparent when we have to add two numbers.

MMCDLXXVIII	2478
MDCCCXLIX	1849

Place-value notation represents on paper the structure which the Romans were already using in their thinking, but not in their notation. It greatly simplifies calculations, which were so difficult in Roman numerals that they were done with the help of pebbles (in Latin, *calculi*).

3 *Promoting reflective intelligence*. It is by the use of symbols that we achieve voluntary control over our thinking, and become able to move from an intuitive to a reflective level in the functioning of our intelligence.[3]

Putting our thoughts into words is not always easy. At an oral level, we can concentrate on putting together the right words in the right order. When we have achieved this, we have not only communicated them to others, but we have a better grasp of our own thinking: a metaphor (i.e. 'grasp') which emphasizes the function of symbols in acting as combined labels and handles for our concepts. This indicates another advantage of co-operative activities in which children talk to each other about the mathematical ideas they are learning. It is also why a good teacher, after an activity in which a new concept has been formed, asks the children to put it into words, and helps them towards a clear formulation.

Writing, though more difficult, takes this process a stage further. It distances us a little from our thinking, allows us to consider it more critically and objectively, and allows us to return to it later for further consideration.

4 *Recording and communication.* If our concern was with the development of a culture, the transition from oral transmission of knowledge and folklore to written records is of such importance that it would come first on our list. In the individual development of a child, this function of writing tends to be used largely as a means for teachers and examiners to try to find out what children have learnt, by getting them to answer questions in writing so that the answers are in a permanent form which can be marked methodically and at leisure. In a book about teaching, the importance of assessment is that we must know how far children have reached in their understanding, to know what they are ready to learn next, or whether revision and/or consolidation are needed before going on. In the case of younger children, it is hard to make reliable inferences of this kind from their written work. Practical and oral work, in which follow-up questions can be put by a teacher, are much better for this purpose.

The benefits which can result from the appropriate use of written mathematics are so great that eventually, written work is indispensable. These benefits will, however, only be gained if this is introduced when children are ready, and in ways whereby children experience the additional powers which it gives. If this is done, then a desire to have something to show will also be fulfilled, and to better effect.

Process and content

One often hears it said, among mathematics educators, that we should emphasize process rather than content. In my view these are interdependent. Good process needs good content, as may be seen from the example already given on p. 79. Almost everyone to whom this is described admires the process. What did this child do? She selected from her repertoire just those numerical relations which were useful for her purpose, and related them in a mathematically elegant way. To do this she had to know these relations, which is to say she had good content. She also needed to have them mentally 'at her finger-tips'. It is hard to say whether this is content or process. Selecting and arranging is certainly process, and since this can be applied to many different contents it is process in a fairly context-free form. But there have to be contents to realize the potential which inheres in this process, and the way it is structured is part of the contents. Structured contents include relationships, as part of their structure. Building well-structured contents is an important kind of good process, and by acting on already structured contents it may add more relationships, in this way making better the contents already there. The relationship is mutually supportive.

Problem-solving is often singled out as an example of process. In terms of the present model, solving a problem is finding a way for achieving a particular goal from a given starting point when we do not have a ready-made plan, and putting this plan into action. This is a situation calling for adaptability, and involves just the same processes acting on just the same kind of content as those described in the previous paragraph. So the foundations of successful problem-solving lie in well-structured relational schemas, together with fluency in a repertoire of useful routines so that conscious attention is free to concentrate on what is unfamiliar. An additional requirement is confidence in one's own ability to cope with new situation. This, and other emotional influences on learning and performance, will then be discussed in Chapter 9.

Can 'learning how' lead to 'understanding why'?

The argument is sometimes advanced that if children are first taught how to do certain mathematical tasks, and are given enough of these to do, understanding will gradually come. While it would be unwise to suggest that this can never happen (someone would certainly find a counter-example), the present model suggests that this would not be a safe principle to adopt as a general basis for teaching unless certain important conditions were satisfied.

In general, understanding results from assimilating new experience to an appropriate schema. Applied to the present discussion, it will result if the new method, first learnt without understanding, is subsequently assimilated to an appropriate mathematical knowledge structure: which must therefore already exist. This being so, the method could have been derived from this knowledge structure; so there needs to be a good reason for not teaching it that way round, either directly, or by helping children to find the method for themselves. Either of these will greatly increase the likelihood of the new method being related to a knowledge structure.

In the approach under discussion, it is natural for children to perceive what they are being specifically taught, namely the use of the methods, as what they are being asked to learn. And if they can get the right answers in this way, why should they bother why the methods work? Though there will always be some children who want to know why, the situation itself is weighted towards rule learning, with all its disadvantages. As teachers, why should we expose children to this risk when it is not necessary?

Though the 'methods first' approach is not advocated as a general approach, there are some instances when 'Here is a method. Why does it work? Will it always work?' can be seen as a valid approach within the present model. These instances need to be carefully chosen, however, and come as extras to the 'understanding first' approach, not as the basis of a desirable teaching method. An example of this kind, which the reader may find intriguing, will be found at the end of this chapter as number 3 of the suggested activities for readers.

Calculators and computers

These have several things in common. First and most important, they manipulate symbols not concepts. They neither store nor process information as such, but symbols which can represent information only in the minds of those who have the right concepts and knowledge structures available. They operate at the level of syntax (relations between symbols), not semantics (relations between concepts).

However, they do these manipulations very fast and very

accurately, and they never grow bored however long, monotonous, and repetitious the tasks.

Calculators

[handwritten: got to know what to do -structs]

These release us from the drudgery of acquiring speed and accuracy in doing complicated calculations. They do not release us from the task of knowing what are the appropriate calculations to do, or whether the answer makes sense. But they make more time available for learning with the emphasis on understanding, and thereby help us to meet this obligation.

They also allow us to choose which methods it is useful for children to learn, and which we may now hand over to calculators. The former include simple routines, fluency in which will enable us to do any job requiring these much faster than if we were to stop and use calculators every time. In the school hall we have set out eight rows of chairs, twelve chairs to a row. Are there enough chairs for 100 people, and if not how many more do we need? We should not need a calculator to answer questions like this one, nor to check our change after a simple purchase. *[handwritten: → appropriateness of case]*

Another category of methods which are still worth teaching includes those which exemplify important mathematical concepts, required in later work, as well as being useful methods in themselves. Long multiplication provides a good example in which we can, if we look for it, see mathematical creativity at work: the construction of new knowledge from existing knowledge. It is no small thing that if we know our multiplication tables from 2 times to 5 times, we can use this information to multiply any two numbers, as large as we care to write.

The first step involves the construction of the tables from 6 times to 9 times, using the commutative property of multiplication. 6×2 is equal to 2×6 which we know already, and so on. This in itself is non-trivial. Not all operations in mathematics are commutative (e.g. subtraction, division), and we need to make sure whether they are or not, or we shall make mistakes.

The next step is in the extension of multiplication to that of a two-digit number by a single-digit number, e.g. 37 multiplied by 4. The method is simple enough. We multiply 30 by 4, 7 by 4, and add the results. Many who have learnt this method do not realize that this depends on another property of the number system, that

$$4(30 + 7) = 4(30) + 4(7)$$

This, generalized, is a basic concept in algebra, known as the distributive property:

$$a(x + y) = ax + ay$$

So by teaching children long multiplication in the right way, we can teach them far beyond the routine itself. We can teach them something about the nature of mathematical creativity, and we can lay some of the foundations of algebra. And since the actual calculations involved in the multiplication of large numbers are much better done by calculator, children no longer need to acquire a high degree of speed and accuracy in doing long multiplications. The time saved can be put to better uses, such as the above. In contrast, I have not found any such benefit in teaching children to do long division, and my preference would be to replace this entirely with the use of calculators.

Another advantage of calculators is that when mathematics is applied to real-life situations, they allow us to work easily with the kind of numbers we are likely to get, rather than with the simpler figures chosen for the examples we give children to learn on.

Thus, rightly used, calculators can help us to improve the quality of school mathematics.

Computers

At present, most primary schools do not have enough computers for individual children to spend more than a short time with them in each week, so they are not as yet to be seen as a major influence on their learning of mathematics. This situation is not without its advantages, since we still need to find out what are the right ways of using them to promote intelligent learning of mathematics. Many programs offered to schools merely replicate existing bad teaching methods. Others simulate practical activities which the children would much better be doing with the physical materials themselves.

Moreover, the software scene is so rapidly changing that many detailed recommendations which might be made are likely to be out of date within a year or two of the publication of this book. Up-to-date information is better sought in periodicals given to this subject.

General principles, however, are more lasting, since they are applications to the particular situation provided by a micro-computer of the principles which have been discussed throughout this book. An example of good computer software would, ideally, provide a well-structured mathematical situation which allowed children to use all of the six modes of schema construction first listed in Figure 4.1, and repeated here because of their importance.

SCHEMA CONSTRUCTION

BUILDING	Mode	TESTING
from our own encounters with the physical world: *experience*	1	against expectations of events in the physical world: *experiment*
from the schemas of others: *communication*	2	comparison with the schemas of others: *discussion*
from within, by formation of higher order concepts: by extrapolation, imagination, intuition: *creativity*	3	comparison with one's own existing knowledge and beliefs: *internal consistency*

Figure 7.3

171

One of the best examples of software which does this is to be found in LOGO, invented by Seymour Papert as a computer language specifically for educational use. Though Papert's thinking developed independently from mine, and in different contexts, the underlying similarity is striking.

Many readers will already be familiar with LOGO. Those who are not will benefit by gaining at least a little acquaintance with it before reading the discussion which follows, and also for its own sake.

The language of LOGO enables the user to control the movements of a screen 'turtle', and to use it to draw patterns, in ways which become increasingly complex and interesting as the user's knowledge progresses. The knowledge needed is of two kinds: of the computer language itself, and of the mathematical structure of the microworld provided by LOGO. 'Microworld' is an evocative term, and though Papert invented it in the context of LOGO, we may apply it to any part of our environment which behaves lawfully; and which can be understood, and in varying degrees controlled, by building a schema representing the system and its laws.

A computer running LOGO provides good opportunity for schema construction in all six of the ways listed above in Figure 7.3.

Mode 1 building. In a typical LOGO learning situation, children are allowed freely to explore the behaviour of the screen turtle in response to the commands typed at the keyboard, single and in combination. Thus they learn by direct physical experience of the LOGO microworld.

Mode 1 testing. Children set their own goals and devise plans of action, in the form of programs, which they predict will draw the pattern or other shape which they want. This prediction is immediately tested when the commands are typed in and the program is run.

Mode 2 building. They learn the commands built into the LOGO languages (known as primitives) by communication, either verbal from their teacher or written from a handbook or instruction sheet.

Mode 2 testing. A good way for children to work is two to a computer, not only because computers are usually in short supply, but for all the benefits of discussion, and co-operative learning, described earlier in this book.

Mode 3 building. The LOGO language allows children to create new procedures, and give them a name, after which the computer will treat this name as a command and execute this procedure whenever its name occurs as part of a program. These new procedures may then be combined to form super-ordinate procedures. For example, a procedure may be invented to draw a shape like the petal of a flower, and called PETAL. Another procedure, called (say) FLOWER, may then arrange a number of petals into a flower; and another, say GARDEN, may scatter flowers over the screen.

Mode 3 testing. All the time one is writing a program or procedure, one is testing by mode 3: whether it fits in with one's existing knowledge of the LOGO environment.

These three modes are more powerful in combination, and LOGO provides a situation which is conducive to this. Devising new programs involves mode 3, as described above. If one is working with a partner, mode 2 testing is thereby introduced; and as soon as the program is run, mode 1 testing also takes place.

As an example of good process, learning with LOGO is outstanding in the field of educational computer software. This is interdependent with good content: LOGO is an elegant language, simple to get started in, but capable of development to complex and sophisticated levels of use. It is also enjoyable, for children and adults alike. These together often produce a halo effect in which the limitations of its mathematical content are overlooked. Unfortunately only a small part of the necessary content of a mathematical curriculum, at primary or secondary level, can be learnt from the LOGO microworld. But the concept of a microworld itself is quite general, and applicable to many other areas within and outside mathematics. And the pioneering work of Papert has provided us with a high-quality exemplar by which to judge other software on offer.[4,5]

Some criteria for a curriculum

There is not space here for a detailed primary curriculum. One such curriculum may be found in my *Structured Activities for Primary Mathematics*. It provides detailed plans of action for teachers based on the theory, and the relation of theory to

173

practice, described in this book.

There is, however, much other material to choose from, so in this brief section are offered some criteria for choice.

   (i) Is there a clear theoretical basis, which takes account of the process of intelligent learning as distinct from the mathematical content?

  (ii) We cannot know for what uses children will need their mathematics in the future world for which we are trying to prepare them. We do not even know what this world will be like. It follows that the most important feature of what they learn is adaptability. This can be provided by helping them to acquire well-structured mathematical schemas, together with a repertoire of widely used routines, experience in adapting their knowledge to new uses, and confidence in their ability to go on doing so. Does the curriculum you are evaluating provide for these?

 (iii) Does the curriculum take account of the hierarchic nature of mathematical knowledge, in which nearly everything children learn builds on past knowledge and prepares for future learning? Is the overall structure to be constructed over the seven years of primary schooling made explicit by concept maps, or in some other equivalent way?

 (iv) Within each topic, is there a progression from concrete to abstract? And are children given practice at re-embodying general concepts in particular instances?

The place of projects and investigations

Both of these have an important place in the mathematical curriculum, provided that they are introduced at the right stages, when children can benefit from them.

One sometimes hears that 'Mathematics is all around us'. This is not accurate: mathematics is in people's minds, a kind of knowledge which can be used in many different ways to understand and organize what is around us. But first we need the knowledge.

To form a new concept, learners need to encounter a number

of examples, fairly close together in time, in embodiments which do not contain too much irrelevant material. Projects do not meet these needs. The mathematics is too dilute: there is not enough mathematical content relative to all other materials, and too much material which does not belong to the concepts to be formed.

The value of projects is after new concepts have been formed and existing schemas enlarged. They provide opportunities for application, call for adaptation of available knowledge, and possibly also provide situations in which there are problems to solve. Children gain experience in the choice of appropriate mathematical models, and of plans of action based on these. These may involve combining ready-to-hand methods with new adaptations specifically devised for the job. Also related to these is the collection and organization of data, in a form which allows the mathematics to be put to use. Environmental studies offer good opportunities for projects of many kinds, and for relating the mathematics learnt in school to the world outside. Children are also using their mathematics in ways similar to those in which they may need to use it in adult life.

For the foregoing, children need already to have appropriate knowledge and skills as a starting point. The sequence in which suitable situations for projects, environmental applications and investigations, are likely to arise is unlikely to be one which meets the requirements, already discussed in detail, for building up mathematically structured knowledge. Mathematical investigations are, however, a different matter, since these can be chosen specifically to fit current states of children's mathematical schemas. Indeed, many of the schema-building activities which appear in *Structured Activities for Primary Mathematics*, and of which a sample is offered in Chapter 6, may be regarded as investigations leading to new concepts. For example, *The rectangular numbers game* invites players to investigate the question: 'Is there some way of predicting whether it is possible for the other player to make a rectangle from the counters I give her?'

By their nature, the mathematical content of investigations of this kind is more concentrated; and in some cases, they can be investigated at different levels of sophistication. One such example is offered as number 6 of the suggested activities for readers at the end of this chapter.

Contents and structure

Summary

1 A mathematical curriculum should provide for the learning of structured knowledge, a good repertoire of routine plans for frequently-encountered tasks, and skills in putting these plans into action easily and accurately.

2 Written work should not be introduced prematurely, before concepts have been introduced by oral and practical work. Used at the right stage, however, written mathematics is indispensable. Among its functions are reducing the cognitive strain of trying to remember long sequences of calculation or reasoning; showing structure; promoting reflecting intelligence; recording and communication.

3 Process and content are interdependent.

4 Calculators release us from the drudgery of acquiring speed and accuracy in doing complicated calculations. They do not release us from the requirement of knowing which are the correct calculations to do, or whether the answer makes sense.

5 Some methods of calculation embody important mathematical principles, and may be worth teaching with this emphasis, while still using calculators as in 4.

6 Computers can be used to provide microworlds for children to explore, using the three modes of schema building and testing already discussed.

7 We do not know what are the uses for which children will need their mathematics when they are grown up. The best preparation for this unknown future is the combination described in (1) above, together with enjoyment of mathematics and confidence in their ability to continue learning it and applying what they already know to new situations.

8 Projects and investigations form a valuable extension of the mathematical curriculum. Projects, in particular, allow teachers to make use of matters of current interest, and provide opportunities for adapting mathematics to new situations, and relating the mathematics learnt in school to the outside environment.

Suggested activities for readers

1 Teach the activity *Cards on the table* to some children.
2 The whole school, consisting of 103 teachers and children, are going on a school trip. They are to be shared between 4 hired coaches. How many persons will there be in each coach? Do the appropriate calculation mentally, and by the use of a calculator. Which gives the more sensible answer? Can you think of other examples in which the answer given by a calculator should not be accepted at face value?
3 (A mathematical investigation.) Here is a method for finding whether a two-digit number is a multiple of 9. Add the digits together, and if the sum is 9, the number is a multiple of 9.
  Example: 36.3 + 6 = 9, so 36 is a multiple of 9.
   (i) Why is this so? (Hint. If you are stuck, draw a number line and, beginning at 9, keep moving to the right 9 at a time.)
  (ii) Does this work for larger numbers, and if so why?
  (iii) (Harder.) Does a similar test apply to multiples of other numbers?
4 (Another mathematical investigation.) Only the first step in the analysis of long multiplication was given in the text. How about 4(30)? Do you know your '4 times' tables as far as four thirties? If not, what other property of a number system is used? Continue the analysis further if you wish, or read about it in detail by following up reference 6.
5 Analyse any mathematical learning activity with which you are familiar in terms of the concept of a microworld.
6 (Another mathematical investigation.) What is the least set of weights by which one can weigh any whole number of grammes up to (say) 100 grammes in a balance (a) with all the weights on the same side (b) with weights on both sides if required?

177

8

Management for intelligent learning

A teacher's dual authority: authority of position, and authority of knowledge

Unless learners accept the authority of their teacher, the teacher cannot function as such. But there are at least two distinct kinds of authority which a school teacher has to exercise, which may be called authority of position and authority of knowledge.

In everyday life these are usually separated. A policeman on traffic duty, a customs officer, the captain of a ship, all occupy positions in which obedience is due to them. In these examples, their powers have the force of law, and disobedience is punishable by fines and/or imprisonment. We can think of other examples of positional authority which, though not enforced by the law of the land, are similar in other respects. A football umpire has the power to award a penalty kick, or to send a player off the field. Here, obedience is required and enforced by the rules of the organization.

In all these cases, the power belongs to the position, not to the person. When persons cease to occupy the positions, they no longer have the powers which go with them. As a spectator, the football referee would no longer be in a position to exercise the powers described; and similarly for the other examples.

In contrast, authority of knowledge is inherent in the persons themselves. Someone who is an authority on growing roses, or the history of the Second World War, remains so whatever their role at a given moment.

Another difference between the two kinds of authority is in our freedom to choose whether we accept their authority or not. With respect to positional authority, we have no choice. When driving a car, we must obey the directions of a policeman on traffic duty. But if as patients we consult a medical authority, whether a general practitioner or an expert on our particular ailment, we are free to choose whether we follow the advice they give. Unlike the first kind, this is a co-operative relationship: and it is of the essence of co-operation that it is voluntary on both sides.

For us as adults, the authority of a teacher is of the second kind. We go to them of our own free will because we believe them to be knowledgeable in a particular subject, and they are free to accept us as students, or not. When we follow their directions, it is because they are helping us to achieve a goal of our own choosing. If we do not want to do the work they give us to do between lessons, they cannot make us. Equally, if they feel that we are not co-operative students, they are free to discontinue teaching us. If there are conditions attached, e.g. about regular attendance, or withdrawal from a course, these will be clearly stated and agreed beforehand.

For children, however, their teachers' authority is both of position and of knowledge. They are in school because the law requires it; they are in a particular teacher's class because either the head teacher, or someone to whom this power has been delegated, has so decided; and their class teacher decides for the most part what they have to learn. Many of us believe that there are good reasons for all these decisions, just as when driving it makes good sense under certain conditions to have someone regulate the traffic. Likewise, an orderly classroom environment is necessary for intelligent learning, and it is part of a teacher's job to create and maintain this. But this does not change the fact that in this part of their authority, the relationship of teachers towards their pupils is a power relationship.

To teach successfully, however, teachers have to be authorities of the second kind, knowledgeable both about their subjects and how to teach these; not to mention other aspects of child development. This is authority of knowledge, not of position; and, as we shall see in the next section, for intelligent learning this needs to be a co-operative relationship.

Obedience and co-operation: their different effects on the quality of learning

A characteristic of a power relationship is that obedience can be enforced by punishment or the threat of punishment. Sometimes it is also encouraged by rewards. The relationship between these and habit learning has already been described in Chapter 2, p. 33, and it will be worth reviewing that section briefly here.

From the extensive literature of the behaviourists, we find that as well as learning reinforced by rewards, animals (typically, rats and pigeons) will learn to do things by which they can avoid punishment (such as electric shocks). They can also be taught habits by symbolic rewards. For example, when a bell has become associated with a food reward, the bell itself acts as a reinforcer. And in the same way, stimuli which have become associated with punishment can be themselves used to produce avoidance learning.

Reward and punishment are powerful methods of bringing about learning in nearly every kind of animal, not excluding our own species. Adults in charge of children are in a strong position to give rewards of many kinds, physical, material, and verbal approval or other symbolic rewards; and to impose punishments of equally many kinds, including disapproval. Learning brought about by rewards and punishment is, however, more likely to be habit learning rather than intelligent learning.

Children are at the most learning age of the most learning species which has yet evolved on this planet. Teaching is an intervention in this process, by which we can greatly help them to use their learning abilities for the greatest benefit of themselves and others *if we know how*. These learning abilities include both intelligent learning and habit learning, and in view of the great difference between these, both in how they take place and in their long-term effects, knowing how begins with an understanding of these differences.

This means that as teachers, it is important for us·(i) to analyse the nature of every learning task, so that we can make a considered decision whether in this case habit learning or intelligent learning is in the long-term interests of the child; and (ii) to choose, or if necessary devise, teaching methods such that the children we teach are likely to bring into use the appropriate kind of learning.

As has already been emphasized, in the learning of mathematics most of the learning needs to be intelligent learning. Habit learning is needed for the number-names and their written symbols. The development of fluency in the recall of useful facts, and of skills in the easy and accurate performance of useful routines, may be thought of as a partnership between habit learning and intelligent learning, in which intelligent learning should dominate.

There are other subjects for which a greater proportion of habit learning is appropriate. For example, I would regard learning to write easily and clearly as a valuable habit. This is likely to remain useful throughout our lives, so lack of adaptability is no disadvantage. For anyone learning to use a computer, I would similarly regard learning to touch-type as a valuable habit to acquire early on, instead of forming a habit of two-finger typing with eyes fixed on the keyboard. But this also illustrates the disadvantages of habit learning, in that we are tied to the QWERTY keyboard, which was designed to minimize the mechanical limitations of early typewriters rather than for ergonomic efficiency.[1] This lack of adaptability of habit learning has proved a major obstacle to improving keyboard design. However, the advantages of good touch-typing skills, in my view, outweigh this disadvantage. These are the kind of considerations to be taken into account, though for other subjects the analysis will be more complex.

Where intelligent learning is the appropriate method, we need to remember that we cannot take over the job of a learner's delta-two. A teacher can, however, greatly help its function by providing a good learning situation and good materials to learn from. Within this environment, an ideal relationship would be one based entirely on co-operation, in which the learner freely consults the knowledge of the teacher, and is also free to learn by the other modes of schema construction summarized in Figure 4.1 (p. 74). When it is their teachers and not the children who have decided what they should learn, we cannot have this ideal situation. Nevertheless, activity methods involving co-operative learning by small groups of children, in which their teacher is involved for some but not all of the time, can come a long way towards it.

The resulting problem, for children and teachers

The problem intrinsic in the dual role of a school teacher is the need to avoid role confusion, and to reduce role conflict as much as possible. This problem would not arise if habit learning were the only kind needed: but we have seen that this is not the case. So the first requirement is for both teachers and children to distinguish between these two roles, and to know which one is active in any given situation.

It is hard for children to do so if their teachers do not. But there are many teachers who treat arithmetical mistakes as if they were a kind of disobedience, and teach children to do as they are told by repetition or reproof rather than by explanation. Since in the long term, habit learning increases the likelihood of mistakes, this role-confusion is counter-productive. The double meaning of terms 'right' and 'wrong' does not help matters. On the one hand they mean ethically right or wrong, 'good' or 'naughty'; and on the other hand they mean correct or incorrect, in the sense of schema testing by the three modes already described, or in the sense of a successful plan of action. This suggests that while teaching it is better to avoid using 'right' and 'wrong' with the latter meanings, but to use 'correct' and 'incorrect' instead; or in some cases, 'I agree' or 'I don't agree'.

Remembering that praise as well as reproof can bring about habit learning, we also need to think seriously about its overuse in situations where the learning goal is the building of structured knowledge. A desire to gain praise from their teacher may lead to an attitude based on 'What does he want me to say?', rather than 'What makes sense in relation to my own knowledge?' In one of the schools where we were field testing activities, it became clear that many of the children were concerned, not with using their own thinking to arrive at an answer which made sense to themselves, but to try to find out what answer we wanted. They were looking at our faces as much as at the materials. This situation has been well described by John Holt in his classic *How Children Fail*.[2]

The achievement of understanding is itself a source of pleasure and satisfaction, as is evident from children's expressions. This is also rewarding to oneself when teaching, and it would seem a cold-hearted suggestion that at these times children and teachers should not share each other's pleasure. However, there does seem to be a possible conflict of principle between this and the argument of the previous paragraph. Reflecting on this, and after discussion with teachers and colleagues working with the project, we have agreed that responses like 'That was a nice piece of thinking', 'You explained that very clearly', are appropriate. These are not rewards for correct answers, but appreciation of intelligent thinking. If children acquire the habit of using their intelligence within the context of mathematics, then surely this is a good habit which they should not need to change.

The authority of the subject

Over a number of years, Buxton has engaged in remedial group work with adults who were convinced that they couldn't do mathematics.[3] One of his techniques involved asking them to visualize a 3 × 3 × 3 cube, as in Figure 8.1.

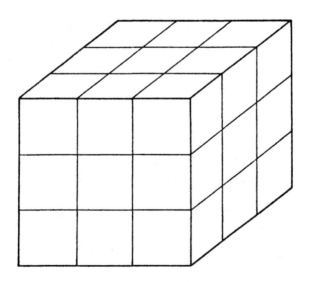

Figure 8.1

They were asked to take time to stabilize this image in their mind (note the explicit removal of time pressure), after which they were given the following problem.

Imagine this cube painted black on the outside. Next, think of it as having been cut up into smaller cubes, each 1 × 1 × 1. How many small cubes have no paint on them?

Once the answer was seen, it was regarded as self-evident by some of Buxton's subjects, needing no confirmation from anyone else. Many, however, so lacked confidence that they remained dependent on his agreement. They were still dependent on their teacher telling them they were right.

Mathematics is a body of knowledge which, though it only exists in people's minds,[4] nevertheless has an existence which is independent of any one person or number of persons, in much the same way as an institution continues to exist although over the years its members change. The truth of a mathematical conclusion depends on its consistency with an accepted body of mathematical knowledge, and both this shared knowledge, and whether a particular statement is consistent with it, cannot be changed by the say-so of an individual. As Buxton has well put it, 'the "authority" is within the mathematics'. In relation to this, teacher and pupil are on equal terms. If a teacher makes a mistake while working on the blackboard, and a pupil points this out, the teacher will correct it. The mathematics itself 'says so'.

What kind of authority are we talking about now? Clearly, it has to be the second kind, authority of knowledge, with the additional force that this is knowledge widely shared and agreed. The basis of this agreement is shared human rationality: shared not only by the great mathematicians of the past and present who have pioneered its construction, but potentially by a majority of children and adults in whom it is part of their genetic endowment. The process can operate on quite a small amount of content, so it can be, and is, found in quite young children: as is exemplified by the third child in observation 1 on page 114.

Management of the learning situation

Here is an illuminating encounter described by Biggs.

> A six-year-old said to me the other day: 'Give me a number and I'll double it for you.' I gave him 37 (he was calculating in his head). He said 'Two thirties that's sixty, two sevens that's fourteen, seventy-four.' He continued, 'Don't tell my teacher.' I asked why not since his method was a good one. The boy answered 'She makes me write it down and I don't understand her method, so I do it in my head and then I write it down her way and I always get my mark, so don't tell her.'[5]

Young as he was, this little boy had learned to manage his learning situation so that he could both use a method he understood, and gain the rewards of obedience. Not all children are likely to be so successful, however. Nor will they need to be, if their teachers can manage the learning situation in such a way that the two aspects of their authority are so far as possible kept distinct. The need for obedience to their teachers, together with reward and punishment in all their varieties, relate to the need for orderly behaviour without which an environment supportive of intelligent learning could hardly exist.

Children are not old enough to know what they need to learn to fit them for the world in which they are growing up. This is, or should be, largely the responsibility of the teaching profession. Teaching them 'tricks for ticks'[6] does not fulfil this responsibility, though it is an easy way of producing short-term results.

We can influence children's learning indirectly, through the power we have over children's learning environment, just as strongly as we can do so directly by telling them exactly what they have to do and how they are to do it. This makes possible a co-operative learning situation of the kind described at the end of the last section.

This is not a book about the sociology of the classroom. The purpose of this short chapter is to show how social factors can strongly influence the quality of learning, and to encourage further thinking and reading in this area. In particular, the present model underlines the effect of perceived role-relationships on the quality of learning.

Management for 'motivation'

It is perhaps unfortunate that the terms 'motivate' and 'motivation' have become widely used, especially the‚ former. For example, 'What is his motivation for climbing the hill?' means no more than 'Why does he want to climb the hill?', or just 'Why does he climb the hill?'

Some possible answers might be 'To enjoy the view from the top', or 'For exercise and fresh air', or 'Because he thinks there will be a good wind for flying his kite.' In terms of the present model, we are asking what goal he expects to achieve by climbing the hill, as is clear from these answers. They do not go easily into the language of motivation: 'He is motivated by a wish to see the view from the top' is better said as 'He wants to see the view from the top.'

These terms seem to stem from behaviourist psychology, in which behaviour is thought to be caused by external stimuli, rather than self-directed. Within this way of thinking (which is not confined to behaviourists), 'motivate' comes to be used as a transitive verb, and motivation takes on the meaning of something which can be applied externally to produce a given action, chosen in this case not by the subject but by the experimenter. Transferred to the teaching situation, this leads to pronouncements such as, 'It is part of a teacher's role to motivate their pupils to learn.' The dubiousness of this statement is concealed by the language. But when translated it becomes 'It is part of a teacher's role to make their pupils want to learn.' How can teachers do this?

Can they make someone want to see the view from the top of a hill, or want to take exercise, or want to fly kites? People want what they want, not what someone else wants them to want. So if I wanted this imaginary person to come with me to the top of the hill, I would have to know the sort of things he liked doing: the goals which gave him pleasure in pursuing. Or, of course, the opposite: anti-goals which he wanted to avoid, such as being left behind and getting lost. This would matter particularly if he were a child.

So if we want children to learn mathematics, we need to know what are their natural goals and anti-goals. Some which it is easy to identify are to gain approval and avoid disapproval from their parents, which in school extends to their teachers. Others are to increase their power over their environment, and to do many kinds of things with other children. In the next chapter it will be suggested that general characteristics such as these have evolved because of their survival value: and the survival value of all the above is easy to see, except perhaps the last, until we view it as learning to co-operate with their peers.

As teachers, we have considerable control over children's environment. We cannot make them want to do any of the above, but assuming that they do, we can determine what they have to do to achieve their goals and avoid their anti-goals. Thus, we can award praise in the form of verbal approval, stars against their names, if they learn what we want them to learn, and also let them experience things they would rather avoid if they do not. This is easy to do, and a powerful means of bringing about habit learning. Under these conditions, learning with understanding may or may not take place.

Fortunately, the desire to understand, to make sense of our environment and thereby to increase our power over it, is not only a very general goal, but one which mathematics can help us to achieve. This is one of its major uses in the adult world, and as we have already seen, we can arrange for children to experience this at their own level in the mathematics they learn at school. Likewise, mathematics has important social value in the complex interactions of commerce and technology which are important to our culture; and it can form the basis of co-operative activities, including games, which provide worthwhile interactions at child level.

If we therefore re-word the misleading question 'How can we motivate children to learn mathematics' with 'How can we manage the school situation so that by learning mathematics, children can satisfy some of their natural desires?', then it can be seen that this is largely what the present book is about.

Summary

1 A teacher's authority is of two kinds, authority of position

187

and authority of knowledge. Outside school these are often distinct.

2 Authority of position embodies a power relationship in which obedience can be enforced by punishment or the threat of punishment, and encouraged by rewards or the hope of these.

3 Authority of knowledge implies a co-operative relationship in which we are free to seek the help of those who are knowledgeable in certain areas, or not; and to follow their advice, or not.

4 Both teachers and children need to distinguish between the two kinds of a teacher's authority, so that the right kind of role-relationships can be used for the two categories of learning needed in school: orderly habits of behaviour, and intelligent learning.

5 Metaphorically, we may also talk about the authority of the subject; that is, of a shared body of knowledge, agreed as a result of human ability to reason.

6 Reward and punishment are conducive to habit learning based on obedience, rather than to intelligent learning based on co-operation.

7 Intelligent learning requires a co-operative learning situation within an orderly school environment.

8 The misleading question 'How can teachers motivate children to learn mathematics?' can be replaced by 'In what ways can teachers arrange that learning mathematics becomes a way by which children can fulfil some of their natural desires?'

Suggested activities for readers

1 Identify some situation in your own experience where confusion between the two kinds of authority described has contributed to lack of success in learning. Note that this confusion may be on the part of children, or teachers, or both.

2 Identify some school situations in your own experience in which the two role-relationships have been clearly distinguished. How was this brought about?

9

Emotional influences on learning

Emotions and survival

Mainstream psychology has tended either to ignore emotions, or to regard them as irrational influences, distractors, which disturb our normal thinking processes. This is in accordance with everyday usage: the *Concise Oxford Dictionary* defines emotion as 'agitation of mind, feeling; excited mental state'. However, I believe that the separation of cognitive from affective processes is an artificial one, which does not accurately reflect human experience. In particular, many students when reflecting on their time at school have reported that strong emotions were aroused by their classroom experiences, and that these greatly influenced their learning for better or worse. As professionals in this area we need a better understanding of these influences than common sense provides. So in the present chapter, I shall suggest how the model of intelligence outlined in Chapter 2 can be extended to include this important influence on our behaviour and learning.

Given that emotions are, subjectively, an important feature of human experience, it seems reasonable to ask whether we should indeed regard them as a disturbance of our normal thinking processes, in which case we should try to minimize their influence; or whether emotions have a useful function, in which case we need to know what this is.

I believe that our emotions, like many other questions relating to human nature and activity, can only be understood by considering them within the perspective of evolution. So we shall begin with a wide-angle view of intelligence in relation to adaptation and survival.[1]

Any species which exists on earth today is here because over the centuries it has evolved physical, behavioural, and mental characteristics which are pro-survival. *Homo sapiens* has become dominant on this planet mainly because of one particular characteristic, intelligence. Why is intelligence pro-survival? Because it gives us the ability to achieve our goal states in a variety of ways to suit a variety of circumstances. Intelligence shows not in behaviour itself, but in adaptive changes of behaviour. Mathematics, as an adaptable and many-purpose mental tool, is an important contributor to these.

If the survival value of intelligence is adaptability, and the survival value of adaptability is that it enables us to achieve our goals, why is this last pro-survival? Because many of our goals are directly related to survival. In some cases the connection is direct and obvious: getting food, finding water, keeping the right body temperature. In others, perhaps, it is less direct.

At the beginning of each day, many of us can be seen travelling by a variety of means to our places of work. When we achieve the goal of this journey we are no better off directly. But this is where we earn the money to pay for food, shelter, clothing, and other necessities of life; so indirectly this goal, and even more so the activities we do there, are pro-survival. When viewed in this way, a surprising number of the goals we seek can be seen as contributing to our survival. Keeping alive is the cumulative result of achieving and maintaining many different goal states: hence the survival value of this ability, in general: and of intelligent learning, in particular.

The above, necessarily brief, overview suggests that if we are looking for a possible answer to the question 'Do emotions serve any useful purpose?', a good place to begin might be by looking for survival value in emotions.

At any time, our senses tell us of many changes in our relationships with our surroundings. Some of these changes take us nearer to, or further from, our goal states, and thus may affect our survival. Others are neutral. So it would be pro-survival in itself to have signals which call our attention to changes which do relate to goal states; and it would also be pro-survival if these signals were qualitatively different from other data reaching our consciousness, since this would enhance their attention-getting quality. This may be recognized as a fair description of emotions. They are hard to ignore, and this is because they are calling our attention to matters which relate to our survival.

Pleasure and unpleasure, fear and relief

The categories of emotion which follow are broad, and within each there are differentiations which I do not make here.

Pleasure

Emotions in this category signal changes towards a goal state. We feel pleasure while eating, taking exercise, resting when tired, enjoying the company of friends. The first three of these examples relate to bodily goal states: nourishment, keeping our muscles strong and our heart and lungs well functioning, physical and mental recuperation. The last relates to the need for mutual help, support, and encouragement, and to the benefits arising from the exchange of ideas in conversation.

The enlargement of our schemas which results from understanding is of very general pro-survival value, since this increases the number of situations in which we can act appropriately. So it is no accident that we feel pleasure when we newly understand something. Here is a student's memory from early childhood.[2]

> When 'reading' the letters of the headline in the newspaper, I suddenly came to the realisation that the words were made up of sound groups I could recognize, which were represented as groups of letters – basically, I had made the discovery that the letters on the chart on my nursery wall were related to the words that I heard people speaking, and that I was attempting to articulate. I had discovered that both were part of the same idea. My mother reports that this discovery sent me racing round the house in ecstasy, attempting to 'pronounce' every written word I came across, and positively gurgling with pleasure.

Unpleasure

This signals changes away from a goal state. We feel unpleasure when we miss our bus, when we lose our purse, or shiver in a cold wind. If at the same time there is nothing we can do about it, we also feel frustration, and all the examples of this kind contributed by my students have come into the latter category.

Fear

This signals changes towards an anti-goal state: that is, one which is counter-survival. It warns us of danger. Thus, we feel fear when our car goes into a skid, or when we encounter a venomous snake. But survival is more than bodily survival, and that which threatens our self-image is also experienced as threatening.

> Fear has been the greatest emotion I have felt in a learning situation. Now, as I reflect on the situations in which I have been afraid, they are all related to a school environment. I have felt this fear as the form-positions are read out – the dread of coming lower than the position I should (in the teacher's opinion) be coming in.

Relief

This signals changes away from an anti-goal state. We feel relieved when the driver of the car we are in regains control after a skid. Again, the threat need not be a physical one.

> I passed the eleven-plus exam, which was an enormous relief to me as I had been expected to. It is an awful amount of pressure for a child that age to be put under. I felt confident I would pass but then feared that would be asking fate to make me fail, so I used to walk home pretending that when the list of passes was read out in class, my name wasn't on it. I did this to practise not crying at the news as a girl had done the year before.

Relief is not the same as pressure, and is a poor substitute for it.

> This cessation of finding pressure in learning something in itself and instead experiencing relief, was also reflected in other areas of the classroom. The results of the tests were used as a basis for seating arrangements. The higher the mark, the further away from the teacher one sat. The unfortunate pupil who had got the lowest mark had the misfortune to sit right under the teacher's nose. Added to this was the shame and humiliation of everyone else knowing your marks.

The foregoing categories are summarized in the diagram below.

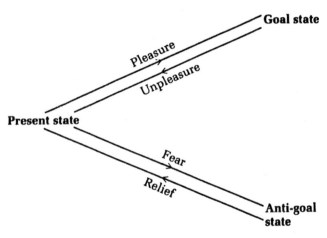

Figure 9.1

Emotions in relation to competence: confidence and frustration, security and anxiety

The first four categories of emotion, described in the previous section, relate to situations which have actually arisen, and call our attention to the need to do something. The next four relate

193

to whether or not we are in fact able to do whatever is necessary to bring about the goal state, and to prevent the anti-goal state. They signal our own competence relative to the situation. This, too, has clear implications for survival, since we need to be cautious about entering situations where we lack competence.

Confidence

Confidence signals competence: ability to move towards a goal state. Most of us, as experienced drivers, feel confidence while driving under normal conditions since we are well able to make the vehicle do what we want.

> English has always been my strongest subject, and so whenever I received a low mark, I felt able to cope with it because I knew I had the ability to do better, reflecting on past marks. A friend however, found the subject difficult and so each 'failure' she found harder to cope with.

Frustration

This results from inability to move towards a goal state. When my computer screen shows uninformative error messages like 'Bad program' and I cannot discover the cause, I feel frustration.

> As long as I can remember I have been better at English than Mathematics: pleasure and confidence in the former and frustration and anxiety in the latter are an integral part of my school experience. Constant frustration in Mathematics has affected, as the model suggests, my ability in attempting certain new tasks. For example, unknown subject areas like computing (which is an important part of my psychology course). My belief in my inability in the Mathematical field has led to basic lack of confidence in an area where I know little, and have no previous experience.

Notice that we are here talking about competence, the ability to achieve one's goal by one's own efforts. If it is a beautiful day, we may well feel pleasure; but we have no confidence in our ability to produce one of these when desired. The relation between these two emotions is well brought out by the next example.

> When I am playing a piece of music on the piano I
> experience pleasure. If I play a wrong note I feel
> unpleasure, but if I quickly correct myself pleasure returns.
> However, if when I play the wrong note, my brother leans
> over my shoulder and says 'F-sharp', I feel frustrated
> because I've been deprived of the chance of moving to the
> goal state by my own efforts.

Security

This signals that we are able to move away, and/or stay away, from anti-goals. A good climber will feel secure half way up a vertical rock face, not because there is no danger, but because he knows that he is in control of the situation.

> From my own experience it appears to be beneficial to do a
> number of questions related to a new concept in order to
> create security and confidence . . . If one feels happy with
> what has just been learnt, there does not seem such a large
> risk involved in going on to the next stage.

Anxiety

If on the other hand we are in a situation where there are possible dangers, and we are unsure of our ability to avert these if they arise, then we are anxious. On an icy road, most drivers will feel anxious even when they are not actually in a skid. This student is describing her feelings during reading lessons.

> As it neared my turn, I became more and more anxious as
> I was unable to do anything about it . . . When it was my
> turn, anxiety was superseded by fear; fear that I wouldn't

195

know all the words, that I'd lose my place or skip a line. I was fearful that the teacher would criticize me for not concentrating, but most fearful that my peers would laugh or think how stupid I was i.e. loss of peer-group status. When I was asked to stop reading, there was a feeling of immense relief.

Learning as a frontier activity

It is in the nature of learning that this takes place in regions where we are not as yet competent.

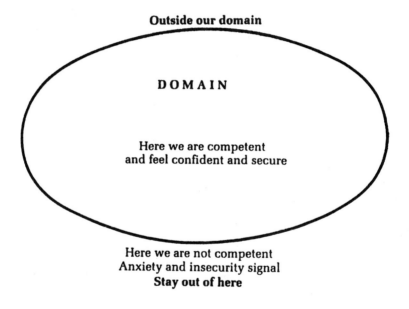

Figure 9.2

In Figure 9.2, the domain represents the region where we can achieve our goals and avoid our anti-goals. This is our region of competence, and within it we feel confident and secure. We might say that we feel 'at home' in a given

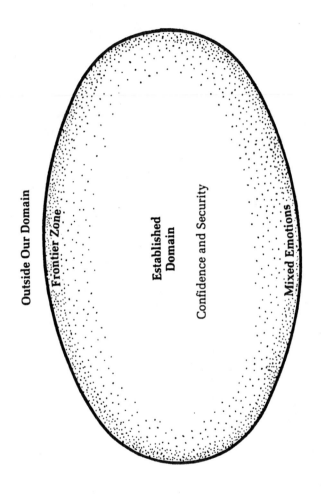

Outside Our Domain

Frontier Zone

Established
Domain

Confidence and Security

Mixed Emotions

Anxiety and Insecurity

Figure 9.3

situation. In the region outside this domain we know that we are not competent. We can neither achieve our goals nor avoid our anti-goals, and feel both frustration and anxiety. Here a person might say 'I'm lost', or 'I'm out of my depth.' These are strong signals to keep out of regions such as these. Ancient maps sometimes warned 'Here be monsters'.

The boundary between inside and outside a person's domain is, however, usually not a sharp one. There is a frontier zone in which we can achieve our goals, and avoid our anti-goals, sometimes but not reliably. It is in this area that learning takes place; and learning is thus a process of changing frontier zone to established domain. The frontier zone then moves outwards, and the process continues. It is pro-survival to expand our domains, so it fits in with this model that we have a strong exploratory urge. Since this takes us into our frontier zones, where we are not fully competent, the model also predicts that mixed emotions are to be expected in these situations: pleasure from success together with increase of confidence, unpleasure from failure and loss of confidence. The latter may be such as to bring learning to a halt, temporarily:

> My brother is six years younger than me and I can remember very clearly when he first managed to take a few steps on his own. When he was 11 months old he tried to stand up on his own, but he fell down and he was really frightened. From that day he wouldn't take another single step. It was five months later . . . that my little brother was persuaded to try again. Fortunately, he managed this time, and although he could not talk, one could see how satisfied and pleased he was with himself by the look on his face. He was obviously very happy and even his eyes were smiling.

Or even permanently:

> I remember, a few years back, I used to envy my sister who could skate. Because it looked such fun, and because I didn't want to remain a spectator all the time, I decided to learn this skill. I was very unsure of the consequences and did not commence my learning with much, if any, confidence at all . . . However, try I did, but no sooner

had I set foot on ice then I found myself with a big crash on the floor, which was a very painful fall. Immediately this put me off, and I did not even attempt to have another go. Needless to say, I've never set foot in an ice-rink since.

Managing children's risks in learning

In both the above examples, one feels that it might have been possible to save the learner from such a severe result of failure. Children learning to ride a bicycle are often provided with a pair of extra wheels, one each side, which prevent them from falling over. Buoyancy aids are provided for children learning to swim. Risks are not only physical, however. Some frustration is bound to be experienced when we cannot always reach our goals. Repeated failure may result in loss of confidence and self-esteem. Teachers can do much to compensate for these negative emotions.

> In the course of my education, I had one teacher in particular who strove to provide this emotional support. He tried to create as relaxed an atmosphere as possible, and tried to encourage everyone to make some contribution, no matter how small, without actually putting pressure on anyone to do so . . . Thus, emotional support was provided by the teacher and by the other pupils.

What a pity that this is not always the case.

> If I did not understand his explanation of a point, instead of explaining it again slowly or in a different way, he seemed to just shout louder and thump his hand on the desk in emphasis of certain points.

The latter approach diminishes ability to think clearly.

> The stress of the situation invariably diminished one's ability to concentrate and think intelligently. Even if you were not the 'victim' at that precise moment, there was still the possibility that you would be next.

This may result in a vicious circle of anxiety leading to failure leading to further anxiety.

> Friday morning was Mathematics, which for me was an awful experience. I panicked and could never get my sums finished and correct . . . Mathematics then meant failure, punishment and ultimately humiliation.[3]

It has been shown experimentally[4] that the functioning of reflective intelligence is diminished by time pressure. Buxton has also shown that questioning by someone in positional authority may be experienced as stressful, and that this in combination with time pressure may produce near-paralysis of rational thinking, accompanied by feeling of panic.[5] In the psychological literature, we read that stress induces a high state of arousal which in turn hinders effective memory function.[6]

From the foregoing, we can derive five basic principles of risk management.

The first of these is to distinguish clearly between the two kinds of authority of a teacher, and help children to do so also. It is appropriate to treat a genuine misdemeanour with disapproval: but errors in something that children are trying to learn are part of the learning situation. With this interpretation, ignorance is not something to hide. Rather, attention is focused on the error, and understanding of this error becomes a sub-goal in itself. By the process of understanding, that which began as error becomes a contribution to knowledge.

The second is to bear in mind that the frontier zone is liable to evoke mixed emotions, in which emotional support from teachers and peers can be a great help.

The third is to allow time for reflective intelligence to function – time to think.

The fourth is to provide opportunities, in the form of time and learning materials, for children to consolidate a new frontier zone, and convert it into established territory, before pushing on into the unknown.

And fifth, we should allow children sometimes to revisit areas in which they are entirely competent and confident. Mathematical games are good for this.

Mixed emotions: confidence as a learner

Learning is a delta-two activity, concerned with improving the abilities of delta-one. The emotional signals summarized in Figures 9.1 and 9.2 will now apply at both levels. Thus, at a delta-two level, we feel pleasure when we make progress towards our learning goal, and frustration when we can make no progress. The pleasure of knowing that our ability is improving may compensate for unpleasure from mistakes at the doing level, or from other sources.

> My father would very often shout, throwing me into a temper, however the pleasure in learning to drive came from my realization that toleration of his temper would eventually mean that I could drive the car single-handed.

A person may be in his frontier zone at a doing level, but comfortably inside his domain as a learner. For example, a pianist who heard a certain piece of music and wanted to play it himself might, on first sitting down at the piano with the written music in front of him, be able to play it only haltingly and with mistakes. As a performer, he would be in his frontier zone. But he would soon form a judgement of his ability to learn to play it well: that is, he would decide whether it was within his domain as a learner. If he decided that it was, he would approach the learning task with confidence, even though *as a performer* he would feel anxious and insecure if suddenly called upon to play the work in public.

This confidence in one's ability to learn is a crucial factor in any learning situation. How long a person goes on trying, and how much frustration he can tolerate, will depend on the degree of confidence he brings to the learning skill initially. His likelihood of success will also depend partly on how long he goes on trying. So a good level of initial confidence tends to be a self-fulfilling prophesy: the learner succeeds because he thinks he can. Lack of confidence will have the opposite effect.

> Some are able to find resources of hope which enable them to view a problem constructively, while others are overcome by feelings of frustration or helplessness. I can

illustrate this observation with my experiences as a student teacher on teaching practice in a local primary school. A lesson plan was drawn up involving the use of language and sentence structure. The children were Asian and, as English was their second language, they were unable to cope with the exercises set for them. One child 'G' remained calm and asked for help and spelling corrections, not understanding any better than the other children, but nevertheless willing to try. Another child 'R' immediately said 'I don't care if I can't do it' and gave up, speaking on the defensive to hide his lack of confidence in his own ability.

The present model also indicates that as teachers we can help to build children's confidence if we distinguish clearly between these two levels, that of performance and that of learning, and help children to do likewise. At the level of knowledge construction, a mistake which by reflection and discussion leads to greater understanding can be as helpful to progress as a successful performance. This is to take a constructive approach to errors. After good understanding has been achieved, together with plans of action based on this, there may be a case for developing skills in performing useful routines fluently and accurately. In this case, the goal is now to minimize errors, so an error itself will result in unpleasure. However, if the number of errors is getting smaller with repeated practice, the pleasure which results from this improvement will outweigh the unpleasure from making mistakes, and again the learner will go on trying.

Confidence in ability to learn has particularly far-reaching consequences, since it will influence whether, for emotional reasons, actual (as against potential) learning ability is increased or decreased. During the long future in which children may need to use mathematics, two of the most influential factors will be whether they enjoyed the mathematics they learnt at school, and whether they are confident in their ability to learn whatever new they need as and when they encounter it.

An important source of this confidence is past experience of success in learning with understanding. With habit learning, any new situation for which the learner has not memorized a rule throws him back on a teacher for new rules. With intelligent learning, however, a learner's cognitive map may already extend part way into the frontier zone. Its features have something familiar about them, which can be understood by expanding and/or extrapolating existing concepts. For example, a child who can count in tens and units is able to see the same pattern repeated in hundreds and thousands. And by extrapolating this pattern in the reverse direction, place-value notation (*if* well understood) can help him to understand tenths and hundredths. In this new context, we see once again the importance of teaching which is based on conceptual analysis and concept maps.

The pleasure of exploration

Exploration involves working within a frontier zone and mapping it. Physical exploration often results in the arrival of settlers, who convert the frontier into established domain. The explorers may then move onward, into a new frontier region.

In the process of schema building, we all have to be explorers, since the constructivist principle, embodied in the present model, tells us that conceptual knowledge cannot be communicated directly. It has to be constructed anew by every learner in his own mind. As Euclid said to King Ptolemy the first, 'There is no royal road to geometry'; nor is there to any other branch of mathematics. With the help of a good guide, however, we may become familiar with what is for us new territory with greater success and fewer hardships than we are likely to do by ourselves. The fact that many pupils fall by the wayside results partly from the shortage of guides who understand the special nature of the region to be explored. It is good also to have companions – fellow learners with whom to discuss what we encounter.

Children, like the young of many species, are natural explorers at a physical level. Particularly characteristic of humans is a proclivity towards mental exploration, which shows itself at an early age. For example, Papousec has shown that infants as young as two or three months show clear signs of pleasure from success in problem-solving, without any material reward.[7] This, together with an innate ability to learn with understanding, forms a powerful combination which has been a major factor in the emergence of *homo sapiens* as (currently) the dominant species on this planet. This urge to explore is not confined to children. I believe that the research scientist in his laboratory and the child engaged in exploratory play have more in common than either has with most school children working for examinations. Any reader who deduces that I am suggesting a more playful approach to the learning of mathematics will be quite right.

The survival value of knowledge does not show at once, and at the time we acquire it we may not even know what we shall use it for. But, like money in the bank, it is good for a wide variety of purposes; and when our immediate needs are taken care of, the pursuit of knowledge has long-term survival value. In acquiring knowledge, we are providing ourselves with a resource from which we can construct a variety of plans of action to serve needs as they arise. Some of these may not have been foreseen when the knowledge resource was being acquired. Like money, gaining it brings pleasure in itself; and, again like money, when we have taken care of the necessities, we can use it to enrich our lives in other ways. 'If you have a loaf, sell half and buy a lily.'

If mathematics is seen as a particularly powerful, adaptable, and multi-purpose kind of knowledge, with aesthetic qualities of its own, the present evolutionary perspective on emotions indicates that with the right kind of guidance, there is much pleasure to be gained while learning it, by children and adults alike.

Summary

1 Emotions are important signals which relate to survival, both physical and in our own self-esteem. Diagrams summarizing some of the main categories will be found on pages 193, 196 and 197.

2 Within our region of competence (domain), we feel confident and secure. Outside this region we feel frustration and anxiety.

3 The boundary between these is not usually a sharp one. There is a frontier zone in which we feel mixed emotions.

4 Learning may be thought of as changing frontier zone into established domain, and therefore takes place in a frontier zone.

5 Mixed emotions are therefore likely to be encountered while learning. If the negative emotions are stronger, a person may give up trying to learn.

6 Emotional support from others can help to keep the balance on the positive side.

7 Stress diminishes the ability to think clearly. Causes of stress in a learning situation include questioning by someone in positional authority, and time pressure. This combination can lead to a vicious circle of anxiety leading to failure leading to further anxiety.

8 The risks inherent in most learning situations can be diminished by good management. Ways of doing this include:

(a) Distingish between positional authority and authority of knowledge.

(b) Provide emotional support for learning.

(c) Allow time to think.

(d) Provide opportunities for consolidating newly learnt material before moving on to new topics.

(e) Allow children sometimes to work in areas with which they are comfortably familiar.

9 A person can be in a frontier zone as a performer, but still comfortably within his domain as a learner. Confidence in ability to learn will support continued efforts to learn, and greatly increase likelihood of success. Lack of confidence will have the reverse effect.

10 Past experience of learning with understanding is an important contributor to confidence as a learner.

11 The urge to explore, both physically and mentally, is an important characteristic of human nature.

12 In their adult life, two of the most influential factors in children's ability to continue using mathematics are whether they enjoyed the mathematics they learnt at school, and whether they are confident in their ability to learn.

Suggested activities for readers

1 Reflect on your own learning experiences, both in and out of school, in relation to the theoretical model described in this chapter.
2 Discuss your own recollections with others who have also followed suggestion 1.
3 For those learning experiences associated with negative emotions, use hindsight to redesign them as you now think they should have been.

10

Continuing professional development

Learning while teaching

Continuing the exploration analogy used at the end of Chapter 9, the present book may be thought of as both a guide to guides, and a guide to explorers.

At the mathematical level, teachers are acting as guides insofar as they understand the maths themselves – though it is common experience that there is nothing like trying to teach something to others for improving one's own knowledge. So the book is intended to help teachers in their roles as guides to young explorers in what Papert has called 'Mathland'. It offers a cognitive map to help in our thinking about the nature of the territory, and of this kind of exploration.

Those learning to be teachers, and those already in the profession wishing to improve their teaching of mathematics, are however more like explorers themselves. The new region to be familiarized and understood is the cluster of related abilities which together characterize intelligence, and which in use are the processes of intelligent learning, together with their applications to the learning of mathematics. Explorations in the area of human intelligence have so far centred mainly on its measurement. Part A of the present book has emphasized its function, and in Chapter 6 suggestions were offered how this exploration might be approached. But this knowledge calls attention to another aspect to be explored, which is particularly the concern of all of us who perceive our work in terms of child development: the nurturing aspect. Hebb[1] has pointed out that we need to distinguish between two meanings of the word 'intelligence', both important. The first, which he calls intelligence A, is an innate potential; the second, intelligence B, refers to comprehension and performance. In biological terms, intelligence A is the genotype, intelligence B the phenotype.

How far, and in what directions, each child develops his or her innate intelligence will be greatly influenced by the quality of the nurture which their intelligence receives, in home and school. This is a frontier of knowledge in which there are still too few explorers. If it is agreed that mathematics is a particularly clear and concentrated example of intelligent learning, then it may also be seen as a good area in which to begin one's own exploration of this frontier.

Chapter 6 was called 'Making a start', with the implied suggestion of continuing this throughout one's professional career. An important part of this process can be done simultaneously with one's own teaching, if we give children activities which embody mathematical concepts in physical materials, and also involve communication and discussion. Just as these provide the children with opportunities for learning by all three modes, so do the children themselves, while doing these activities, provide us as teachers with embodiments of intelligent learning which we can observe in action, discuss with colleagues, and which provide a starting point for our own creativity as teachers. In this way we get 'two for the price of one', time-wise. What is more, as our own theoretical grasp increases, we find that our classroom observations increase in depth; and our discussions also gain by being related to a shared theoretical schema. So our own learning follows a rising curve.

The need for professional companionship

While there is no substitute for doing structured mathematical activities with children as a foundation for one's own learning, it is not cost-effective in time to have to find out everything for oneself. Modes 1 and 2 are more powerful when used in combination; and knowledge has the benevolent property that however much we give to others, we still have as much ourselves. For this reason alone, it is a great help to have at least one companion while exploring a new approach to teaching mathematics.

A B

Figure 10.1

But the difficulty of 'going it alone' arises not only from the lack of opportunities for discussion, but from a more subtle process which was strikingly demonstrated in a classic experiment by Asch.[2] This was disguised as an experiment in perceptual judgement. The subject sat at a table with a group of others whom he thought were also subjects, but who in fact were accomplices of the experimenter. Figure 10.1 shows two of the kind of stimuli which were used.

After looking at display A, the subjects had to choose from display B the line which was of the same length. They all sat round a table together, and in turn stated their decisions aloud, the actual subject being in the last-but-one position. On most of the trials, all gave the same answer, since the task was an easy one. But on some of the trials, the confederates had all been told beforehand to give the same, incorrect, answer. The real point of the experiment was to see whether, under this social pressure, the genuine subject would give, not the answer which was obvious to his perception, but the socially conforming incorrect answer. Under these conditions, about 74 per cent of the subjects conformed at least once; and about 32 per cent of all the answers by the (genuine) subjects conformed. If the effect of majority opinion is as strong as this under conditions where the correct answer was clear to see, we may expect it to be even stronger in cases when the choice is much less obvious, as it is when trying to choose the best teaching approach.

This experiment has since been repeated with variations by many other investigators. One noteworthy discovery was that if just one of the accomplices departed from the majority choice, conforming answers by the genuine subject dropped to about 6 per cent.[3]

Taken together with the positive benefits already discussed, these findings suggest that the advantages of having at least one companion within the same profession for one's explorations of new and better ways of teaching mathematics are considerable.

Some rewards of intelligent teaching

The pleasures of mental exploration have already been seen in relation to the survival value of knowledge. And it may be worth repeating that although this may have been the cause of the development of intelligence to such a high degree in *homo sapiens*, now that we have it we can use it to enrich our lives in other ways.

In the teaching profession, one of these enrichments is that of seeing the illumination which results from understanding. When watching children's faces, it is so like a light being switched on that one almost forgets that this is a metaphor. But once having experienced it, one wants to see it happen again. Teaching in ways which bring children's intelligence into action has the effect that they too want to continue the pleasures of expanding their knowledge and understanding; and so human interaction can happen of a kind which, coupled with the knowledge that we are also contributing to the children's long term benefit, makes all the hard work involved more than worth the effort.

Summary

Many years ago when I was first appointed as an assistant lecturer at Manchester University, I found the following on a brass plate near the entrance to the main (and oldest) building. To my regret, it has since disappeared from there, though not from memory. I ask the reader's indulgence for my reproducing it here, instead of a more conventional summary to this last chapter.

Those who learn from one who is still learning
    drink from a running stream.
Those who learn from one who has ceased to learn
    drink from a stagnant pond.

Notes and references

Prologue: Relational Understanding and Instrumental Understanding

1 *Mathematics Teaching* (Bulletin of the Association of Teachers of Mathematics), 77, December 1976.
2 R. R. Skemp, *Understanding Mathematics*, book 1, London, University of London Press, 1964.
3 For a fuller discussion of this, see pp. 82–84 in the present book.
4 However, it was recently pointed out to me that for some pupils, this pleasure is offset by feelings of insecurity resulting from not knowing why the method gave the right answers.
5 I would not put it quite like this today. Experienced mathematicians are fluent in a repertoire of routines which they can do with a minimum of conscious attention. Relational understanding is still there if needed.
6 See note 5.
7 This was written before the present efforts to improve methods of examination.
8 H. Bondi, 'The dangers of rejecting mathematics', *Times Higher Education Supplement*, 23 March 1976.

1 Why is mathematics still a problem subject for so many?

1 W. H. Cockcroft (Chairman of Committee of Inquiry), *Mathematics Counts*, London, Her Majesty's Stationery

Office, 1982, p. 6, para. 16.
2   Cockcroft, op. cit., p. 10, para. 34.
3   S. J. Eggleston, *Learning Mathematics*, APU Occasional Paper No. 1, London, DES, 1983.
4   D. Foxman, G. Ruddock, L. Joffe, K. Mason, P. Mitchell, and B. Sexton, *A Review of Monitoring in Mathematics 1978 to 1982*, London, HMSO, 1986.
5   K. M. Hart *et al.*, *Children's Understanding of Mathematics: 11–16*, London, John Murray, 1981.
6   H. Whitney, 'Taking responsibility in school mathematics education', in L. Streefland (ed.), *Proceedings of the Ninth International Conference for the Psychology of Mathematics Education*, vol. 2, State University of Utrecht, 1985.
7   It was Euclid who said to Ptolemy the first, when he asked for an easy way, to learn geometry: 'There is no royal road to geometry.'
8   R. R. Skemp, *Intelligence, Learning, and Action*, Chichester and New York, Wiley, 1979.
9   'Theory is in the end . . . the most practical of all things.' J. Dewey, *Sources of a Science of Education*, New York, Liveright, 1929.
10 S. H. Erlwanger, 'Case Studies of children's conceptions of mathematics – Part 1', *Journal of Children's Mathematical Behavior*, I, 3, Champaign, Ill., Study Group for Mathematical Behavior, 1975, p. 93.

2 Intelligence and understanding

1   R. R. Skemp, *Intelligence, Learning, and Action*, Chichester and New York, Wiley, 1979, pp. 41–50.
2   R. R. Skemp, *The Psychology of Learning Mathematics*, Harmondsworth, Penguin, 1971, p. 14; 2nd ed., 1986, p. 14.
3   Ibid., p. 46; 2nd ed., p. 43.

3 The formation of mathematical concepts

1 H. Poincaré (trans. G. B. Halstead), 'Mathematical creation', in B. Ghiselin (ed.), *The Creative Process*, New York, Mentor, 1955, p. 33.

2 J. Wrigley, 'The factorial nature of ability in elementary mathematics', paper read to N. Ireland branch of the British Psychological Society, 17 November 1956, abstract in *Bulletin of the British Psychological Society*, May 1957.

3 N. Weiner, *Cybernetics*, New York, Wiley, 1943.

4 K. W. Gruenberg and A. J. Weir, *Linear Geometry* (2nd ed.), New York, Springer-Verlag, 1977, p. 10.

4 The construction of mathematical knowledge

1 Buddleia, sometimes known as the butterfly tree, is recommended for those who like to see butterflies in their gardens.

2 For a good discussion of this and other aspects of children's learning, see H. Ginsberg, *Children's Arithmetic: The Learning Process*, New York, Van Nostrand, 1977.

3 For further discussion of the importance of talk and discussion, and other matters relating to classroom organization for learning in the ways described in the present book, I highly recommend Tom Brissenden's new book *Talking about Mathematics: Mathematical Discussion in Primary Schools*, Oxford, Blackwell, 1988. This was published after the present book had gone to press: otherwise, I would have referred to it at much greater length.

4 For a detailed account of this experiment, see R. R. Skemp, 'The need for a schematic learning theory', *British Journal of Educational Psychology*, xxxii, 1962. A shorter but more accessible account may be found in R. R. Skemp, *The Psychology of Learning Mathematics*, Harmondsworth, Penguin, 1971, pp. 40–2; 2nd ed., 1986, pp. 38–40.

5 E. T. Bell, *Men of Mathematics*, Harmondsworth, Penguin, chapter 19.

6   A full explanation of the ideas of a fraction and of fractional numbers would take many pages. Two such explanations can be found elsewhere; at adult level, in Skemp, op. cit. (note 3), 1st ed., pp. 186–96 and 2nd ed., pp. 174–84; and at child level, in R. R. Skemp, *Structured Activities for Primary Mathematics*, Vol. 2, London, Routledge, 1988, the whole of network Num. 7.

7   Here is an example for those who are already familiar with matrices as representing a geometric transformation (such as a translation). Here we might start with a line as operand, and apply a reflection to this line, and then a second reflection to the result. The matrix which represents the transformation (in this case a rotation) equivalent to the combination of these two translations is what is meant by the product of the two other matrices; and the (rather strange) way in which this product is obtained from the original two matrices is what is meant by multiplication of matrices. Even in this advanced example, the meaning of 'multiplication' is not a reconstruction but only an expansion of the original schema for multiplication, as here presented.

8   M. Luft, unpublished third year honours psychology project, Manchester University, c. 1970.

9   My colleague in these visits was Janet Ainley, now Lecturer in Primary Mathematics, University of Warwick.

10 R. R. Skemp, *Intelligence, Learning, and Action*, Chichester and New York, Wiley, 1979, Chapter 1.

5 Understanding mathematical symbolism

1   R. R. Skemp, *The Psychology of Learning Mathematics*, 2nd ed., Hardmondsworth, Penguin, 1986, Chapter 4.

2   A recent and useful contribution to this field may be found in D. Pimm, *Speaking Mathematically*, London, Routledge & Kegan Paul, 1987.

3   Condensed from R. R. Skemp, *Intelligence, Learning, and Action*, Chichester, Wiley, 1979, pp. 131–41, where a more detailed discussion of this model can be found.

4   D. O. Tall, 'Conflicts and catastrophes in the learning of mathematics', *Mathematical Education for Teaching*, 2,

Notes and references

4, 81, 1977, pp. 2–18.
5   For further reading on this subject, I recommend the classic work of L. S. Vygotsky, *Thought and Language*, Cambridge Mass., MIT Press, 1962.
6   Twenty-five is a quarter of a hundred.

6 Making a start

1   J. N. Ainley, personal communication, 1988.
2   H. Gardner, personal communication, 1988.
3   R. R. Skemp, *Structured Activities for Primary Mathematics*, London, Routledge, 1989.

7 The contents and structure of primary mathematics

1   R. Rees, personal communication, 1985.
2   W. H. Cockcroft (Chairman of Committee of Inquiry) *et al.*, *Mathematics Counts*, London, HMSO, 1982, p. 89.
3   See chapter 5, pp. 92–93. For further discussion of this important topic see also R. R. Skemp, *The Psychology of Learning Mathematics*, 2nd ed., Harmondsworth, Penguin, 1986, the whole of Chapter 3; and Skemp, *Intelligence, Learning, and Action*, Chichester, Wiley, 1979, Chapter 11, sections 11.6–11.12.
4   S. Papert, *Mindstorms*, Brighton, Harvester, 1980.
5   A good introduction to the use of LOGO in the classroom is provided by J. N. Ainley and R. N. Goldstein, *Making Logo Work: A Guide for Teachers*, Oxford, Blackwell, 1988.
6   Skemp, 1986, op. cit., pp. 154–61.

8 Management for intelligent learning

1   On the early mechanical typewriters, keys of letters which often came next to each other in words were spaced apart, to reduce the likelihood of jamming when typing fast.
2   John Holt, *How Children Fail*, London, Pitman, 1965. (Also available as a Penguin.)

3   L. G. Buxton, 'Cognitive-affective interaction in foundations of human learning', unpublished doctoral thesis,
Warwick University, 1985. See also L. G. Buxton, *Do
You Panic about Maths?* London, Heinemann Educational, 1981.

4   There are those who think that mathematics has an
existence of its own, independently of human minds.

5   E. E. Biggs, 'Investigational methods', in L. R. Chapman
(ed.), *The Process of Learning Mathematics'*, Oxford,
Pergamon, 1972, pp. 232–3.

6   I have borrowed this apt description from Judith Bamford
(personal communication, 1988).

9 Emotional influences on learning

1   For a more detailed treatment, see R. R. Skemp,
Intelligence, Learning, and Action, Chichester, Wiley,
1979, Chapter 2.

2   This and the other extracts quoted inset in this chapter
have been contributed by students taking my course *Foundations of Human Learning* at Warwick University. They
have agreed to my quoting them, anonymously; and I am
grateful to them for this valuable collection of examples.

3   Mathematics was more frequently linked with negative
emotions in these students' recollections than in all other
school subjects put together.

4   R. R. Skemp, 'Difficulties of learning mathematics by
children of good general intelligence', unpublished
doctoral thesis, Manchester University, 1958.

5   L. G. Buxton, 'Cognitive-affective interaction in foundations of human learning', unpublished doctoral thesis,
Warwick University, 1985. And see also L. G. Buxton,
Do you Panic about Maths?, London, Heinemann Educational, 1981.

6   W. Hockey, *Stress and Fatigue in Human Performance*,
Chichester, Wiley, 1983.

7   H. Papousec, 'Individual variability in learned responses
in human infants', in R. J. Robinson (ed.), *Brain and
Early Behaviour*, London, Academic Press, 1969.

10 Continuing professional development

1   D. O. Hebb, *The Organization of Behaviour*, New York, Wiley, 1949.

2   S. E. Asch, 'Effects of group pressure upon modification and distortion of judgement', in E. E. Maccoby, T. M. Newcomb, and E. L. Hartley (eds), *Readings in Social Psychology*, New York, Holt, Rinehart & Winston, 1958.

3   V. L. Allen and J. M. Levin, 'Social support and conformity: the role of independent assessment of reality', *Journal of Experimental Social Psychology*, 7, 1971, pp. 48–58.

Index

Printed in the United Kingdom
by Lightning Source UK Ltd.
104863UKS00001B/11